Freedom Press International Inc.
12-111 Fourth Ave., Suite 185
St. Catharines, ON L2S 3P5

Printed in the United States of America

Cover Design: Clara Fama



ISBN: 978-1-927684-13-9

## Acknowledgements

- To my wife Angela, you are first and foremost the greatest gift I have received in my life. I have come to know the Love of God out from the ethereal and into reality by your love and grace. Thanks for your vision of this work and your encouragement to accomplish it.
- To Alisha, Jotham and Isaac, God's trail blazers for the next generation. Thanks for letting Daddy disappear time and time again to work on this manuscript.
- To Mary-Ann Meyer who had every good and true reason to not be available to give of her time and expertise in editing and yet volunteered anyway. Thank you for all the wise words, practical insights, professional wisdom and words of encouragement.
- To my Sister in Law Clara for her exquisite work on both the front and back cover.
- To the Lord Jesus Christ, I am overwhelmed at your great love, I am speechless and stand in awe when I consider how You have carried me and how You carry me forward. Above all else be glorified.

## Table of Contents

# Cornerstone Truths for the Christian Life

## The Preface

King Solomon commented that there is no end of books, they will just keep coming and coming and coming. Having worked in a book store I can promise you that Solomon had it right there is no end of books. So why should I add another book to the ever increasing pile?

Can you remember your salvation experience? For me, everything that could change in my life changed in that instance. The reality of a 'born again' experience was mine; the reality of being a new creation would be the only way that my life could be described. Heaven came down and glory filled my soul, my life was changed forever, God was revealing Himself to me on a daily basis. My devotional life was the most significant and glorious event of my day, every day. Though no one told me what to do or how to do it I found myself embarking upon a discovery of God and of biblical foundations of how to meet with God. As I look back after walking with God for forty one years I can see how the foundations laid in my life have been a blessing to me and to many thousands of people that I have been able to minister to in different parts of the globe.

I came to write this devotional through the encouragement and prompting of God on my heart and through the persistence of my wife. Her faith in me and my ability to communicate the truth of God to people with a pen was greater than mine. Having been blessed to be in full time ministry for 21 years and to enjoy cross cultural ministry as a missionary in Uganda, East Africa; I had become accustomed to communicating the Word of God through preaching and teaching. As a minister of the gospel there is always a burden on your heart to ensure that people are coming to faith in Christ and to ensure that their spiritual foundation is secure. I was uncomfortable with trying my hand at communicating through the written form. God graciously used my wife to prod me to unburden my heart with pen and paper.

Every day there are new people giving their lives to Jesus and starting the walk of faith and every day Christians are seeking to deepen or revive their relationship with God. Many times both groups have not been discipled in the spiritual disciplines and that results in their Christian experience being neither fulfilling nor enriched with the presence and power of God. The purpose of this devotional is to lay a solid biblical foundation of the most important cornerstone truths for the Christian life so that both new believers and awakening Christians can fulfill their calling and purpose. That is why I choose to add another book to the ever increasing pile for I have a profound confidence that within these pages believers will meet with God and be transformed, re and trained.

## The Introduction

You may have already purchased Cornerstone Truths for the Christian Life or you are looking through this introduction to see what the content of the book is. The book is actually better described as a devotional. It is not to take the place of your daily bible reading but to come along side of it and to assist you in growing in and hearing from God. It is written with the purpose to speak to both your heart and your mind increasing your hunger and thirsting for God and His will for your life. The devotional is broken up into four month sections. Each month covers a specific spiritual truth that we will put under the microscope to learn from.

***First Month - The Believer's Identity*** – When we see who we are, when we know our significance and we understand our purpose we will attain God's destiny for our lives. In this month we will look at 31 Biblical truths concerning our identity in Christ that will answer the question of our significance and our purpose.

***Second Month - The Believer's Communion*** – Believers commonly ask - What is prayer? How do I pray? Why are my prayers not being answered? How do I pray the will of God with assurance? Learning to pray the way Jesus prayed will not only answer these questions it will teach us how to live in communion with God.

***Third Month - Jesus – The Believer's Lord*** – I know about Him but do I really know Him? Why does He have so many names, so many titles, what do they all mean to me and the world I live in today, how do His names and titles change my world and the world of today? Come into this month with an open heart and have a greater revelation of your Lord and Christ.

***Fourth Month - The Believer's Manual*** – The means by which each and every believer can attain full growth and maturity is by living in obedience to God's manual for life. As we begin to uncover the wisdom and relevance of God's word to us we can uncover God's will in all circumstances and situations. This month gives practical direction for rightly responding and researching God's word.

Each day the devotional ends with a prayer that is focused specifically on incorporating the lesson into the life of the believer. Each devotional is written with the perspective that change only occurs in life because of the choices we make. At the end of each week there is a scripture to be memorized and questions to be answered to aid in the process of your transformation.

Your Commitment - Make a commitment today to not miss a day without reading in this devotional. Growth takes place imperceptibly, day by day by day as the right nutrients are in place. The same is true spiritually in our lives when we discipline ourselves to do what is the most essential. Building a spiritual foundation takes time but once it is built it will last for a lifetime that leads to eternity. Make a commitment now to daily walk with God with this devotional and I know you will be richly blessed.

This project has been bathed in prayer, the heart behind writing this devotional is the love affair that God has called all of us into with Himself. That love affair that God has with you is what I desire you too experience afresh and anew as you set time aside to meet with Him. As the days flow by my prayer is that you will meet with God in life altering, life changing ways that enable you to live in freedom and fulfill God's will for your life.

## The Believer's Identity

### Day 1

### Just as Righteous as Jesus

For our sake He made Christ [virtually] to be sin who knew no sin, so that in and through Him we might become [endued with, viewed as being in, and examples of] the righteousness of God [what we ought to be, approved and acceptable and in right relationship with Him, by His goodness]. 2 Corinthians 5:21 (Amplified )

Today, let's take a minute and reflect on the great salvation that has been attained for us. This next year is going to be a year unlike any other year you have known in your life. It is going to be a year of discovering who God is, how much He loves you, the grandeur and the splendour of His personality, the magnificence of answered prayer and the great truths of His Word.

We start today with a foundational thought that will be a strength to you every day of your new life with God. Your Lord and your Saviour became sin for you. He became the most wretched thing in the universe that He might purchase you with His own blood. He, who never sinned, became sin.

In this day and age, not only do people deny the existence of God, they also deny His moral perfection. But without dealing with the issue of sin, no true salvation can take place. Jesus' horrific death is a testament to the penalty of sin, for sin brings death and separation, but through Jesus' one-time sacrifice, we are now viewed from heaven as the righteousness of God. This is God's divine exchange ministry in full effect. God removes our sin as far as the East is from the West (Psalm 103:12). When we receive His righteousness, God removes the penalty of death that we fully deserve and we receive eternal life with God forever (1 John 3:14). Our filthy garments are replaced with glorious robes of righteousness. He gives joy for sorrow, dancing for weeping and so much more (Isaiah 61:3).

We can declare with full assurance, "My sins are washed away and I am well pleasing to my Father. There is not one sin associated with my name; I am as righteous as Jesus in the Father's eyes."

*O Daddy, I have so much to thank You for. I am overwhelmed at the thought of Jesus' great sacrifice for me. I am so thankful and so grateful for the love that You have for me in sending Him to die in my place. Open my eyes that I might see You more, know you more and love You more. I give You this New Year with hope and with faith as You are working in my life, in the name of my Lord and Saviour Jesus Christ.*

## Day 2

### My Adoption is Complete

**For you did not receive a spirit of slavery to fall back into fear, but you received the Spirit of adoption, by whom we cry out, "*Abba*, Father!" The Spirit Himself testifies together with our spirit that we are God's children**" Romans 8: 15, 16

This month of study is entitled "The Believer's Identity" because, according to the Word of God, you have been "born again" or "born from above". You are a new creation through your faith and trust in what Jesus did for you on the cross. Throughout this month, we will examine spiritual truths that speak to your new identity in God. Healing and wholeness will come to your soul and life as you trust in God's declarations of who you are.

You and I are to now live the life we were originally intended to live. We are not just the product of our race, chance or our parents' union. We were planned and purposed by God to know Him and to love Him (John 1:12, 13). He is our ultimate source and life-giver and He calls us sons and daughters. We are not children of God by creation; we are children of God by adoption (Romans 8:15). We are His own dear children, dearly beloved sons and daughters of the Father of the universe who has a glorious plan and purpose for our existence.

Religion taught us to fear God in a negative way. We approached God trying to convince Him to favour us, bless us and meet our needs. But Jesus came and presented God as Daddy; He continually spoke of God in intimate personal terms and, in so doing, opened our eyes to know that the heart of God is the heart of an absolute intimate, loving, personal Father. As you approach Him in prayer and in worship remember this: He adopted you; He gave you His very own name; you are His dearly beloved; and He loves to hear your voice and to spend time with you (Song of Solomon 2:14). Let your heart rest in His great love for you and freely bring every concern you may have to Him (Psalm 55:17).

Take a minute and picture a scale, on one side of the scale is the riches of the universe, this would include every precious, priceless and spectacular thing. Now on the other side of that same scale is you and only you. If the scale were made to measure what has incalculable value in the eyes of God, it would be your side of the scale that would CLANG throughout eternity. For God has proven the measure of His love for you and me by sending His Beloved Son to take our place. Our adoption is complete, His love is assured and our status is confirmed. Now it is time to throw an internal party of celebration at the great love shown to us.

*Daddy, I am Your child and it is great to come into Your loving presence. How awesome to consider that I have been adopted into Your great family. I no longer will live by fear or try to earn what You have so painstakingly provided for me. How spectacular to think that you treat me as Your very own child!*

## Day 3

## I am His Child by Covenant

**"But to all who did receive Him, He gave them the right to be children of God, to those who believe in His Name."** John 1:12

This verse tells us that Jesus must be received. We must take Him as our own Saviour and Lord. It is similar to a marriage relationship. I had to ask my betrothed if she would take me, my name, my good and my bad, my past and my future and be joined to me. She had to say yes—yes to the ring, yes to my name and yes to my very essence. The Christian marriage vow is not an "I do" but an "I will", meaning I will fulfill this vow that I make before God and these people. The "I will" seals our marriage covenant. My spouse is no longer just who she was; her name change signifies her accepting of me, receiving of me and giving of herself. This act enabled a new family to begin with the potential for more persons to be born into that family name.

Salvation is similar. Jesus name, His good (for He has no bad), His past and His future—all He has to give are made available. It is based on a covenant commitment of confession, repentance and loyal love. He did His part on the cross; now we do our part and as we receive Him as our one and only God and King. He gives us the right and authority to be called His very own children. We take on His name and become a part of His family. No devil in darkness, no terrible circumstance, no trouble of any kind can erase the truth of our family name and relationship (Romans 8:38-39). We are children of God. He calls us His own.

What you own, you care for, love and protect. There is a difference between caring for something that belongs to someone else and caring for something that is your very own. Through salvation and adoption, we become God's very own prized possession. My father passed away when I was nine and anything that was his immediately became prized; the older I get the more precious those things become. They may have no literal value, but to me they are without price. They mean something to me because they meant something to him and they connect me to him.

How much more is that true for God and you? You are covered with the very blood of His Son and filled with the person of the Holy Spirit; you are indwelt by Him and you live and move and have your being through Him. God has placed authority within you to reveal to the world around you that you are His very own prized possession. Nothing has the power to cancel out what God has declared.

*Lord Jesus thank You for Your love for me, it is so enriching to consider Your great love to me.*

## Day 4

### His Personal Love Slaves

**"Don't harm the earth or the sea or the trees until we seal the slaves of our God on their foreheads."** Revelation 7:3

If I were to ask you whose slave you are, what do you think you would answer? Most likely you would say to me that you are no one's slave or, at the very least, that you are your own master. And yet, the Bible declares that we are slaves to the one we obey. If we submit to sin then it is our master; if we submit to Christ, then He is our Master. Though we are His children by adoption and His heirs by lineage, we are slaves as well—love slaves, make no doubt about it, but slaves nonetheless.

You and I have been bought with a price, paid in full with one sacrifice so that we might be God's own possession, fully owned and looked after by Him. What a peace and a joy it should bring to our hearts to know that God so intimately looks after us as His own possession. Paul introduces himself in almost all of his books as an apostle and slave of Jesus Christ. Though Paul fully understood his adopted status, he also understood that to be a love slave of God is required protocol.

In Old Testament law, it was forbidden for a Hebrew to own another Hebrew. One of the reasons that God forbade it was because the Israelites had been slaves in Egypt. When people came into financial crisis, however, they would indenture themselves as servants. This means that, for a certain period of time, they would work as a servant in the home of a fellow Hebrew until they had earned enough to either free themselves, pay their debts or until the next year of Jubilee.

All slaves were to go free at the time of Jubilee and have their inheritances and property returned. In some cases, however, indentured servants would agree to stay on. They did this out of love—not just their love for their masters, but because of their masters' love for them. When a servant/slave saw that their master loved them and their family, truly had their best interests at heart, looked after them and could ensure a better way of life, then they would become a love slave. In doing so they would pierce their ear and would be known for the rest of their lives as a love slave.

Psalm 40:6, a prophetic psalm fully understood to be Jesus proclaiming the Father's way of life, says that "a body you have prepared for me and my ears you have opened." Interestingly enough, the word "opened" is the Hebrew word "to dig and to bore", a process that is endured when one's ear is pierced to create a love slave. Jesus was most definitely the perfect love slave, who never disobeyed His Father's will, even to the point of death. If Jesus, the Son of God, was also God the Father's love slave, should we desire to be anything less?

*Daddy, who can love me like You, who knows me so perfectly and yet loves me so dearly? You have a million reasons to leave and yet You have covenanted to stay. Your love for me is beyond words and no one but You could take care of my every need. I gladly go to Your door that I might be marked as your love slave for eternity.*

## Day 5

## I am an Heir of the Kingdom

**The Spirit Himself testifies together with our spirit that we are God's children and if children, also heirs – heirs of God and co-heirs with Christ – seeing that we suffer with Him so that we also may be glorified.** Romans 8: 16, 17

Being called an heir interests me on a number of different levels, culturally, personally but most importantly because of Who is giving the promise.

Many families have learned the secret of passing an inheritance generationally. A wise man provides for grandchildren through inheritance both naturally and spiritually (Proverbs 13:22). If it is true in the natural realm that fathers and mothers desire to provide an inheritance for their children, how much more true in the spiritual realm!

My Father is a King, His Son is King of Kings, and they possess the only eternal Kingdom of light, righteousness, glory, power, justice and holiness. The earth is the Lord's (Psalm 24:1) and the universe is the Lord's (Genesis 1:31-2:1). As King over it all, He shares His rulership with His children. We are co-heirs with Jesus (Romans 8:17). Does it stir your heart as it does mine? Are the possibilities endless? What a family to be a part of! You and I are heirs of God's Kingdom!

Being an heir means you are entitled to something that no other person is entitled to. That should give you a sense of significance and importance. I received a letter from the National Defence of Canada when I turned eighteen. This letter informed me that my father had taken money from his paycheck and put it aside to ensure that his children would receive a stipend to assist them with college and university. Words cannot express what went off in my heart as I read that letter. I was overwhelmed with my father's love and thoughtfulness. He had me on his mind—my future, my education—and he did something to assist me even though he had been deceased for ten years.

For all the great dads out there who have made preparations for their children's future in both natural and spiritual terms, what a testimony of true love! God, the ultimate Father, gave His only Son for us and through Him, our inheritance is greater than we could ever imagine!

*Father, by your Spirit I will live up to my family name and in Jesus, right now, I am a child that makes your heart proud and overflowing with joy. I so look forward to the day when I hear You say, "Well done, My good and faithful servant. Enter into My joy forever and ever and ever." I believe I can taste that even now. I am growing in my excitement at how awesome Your plans are for my life. I put my trust in You and You alone.*

## Day 6

### I am a Student of Truth

**"The disciples were called Christians first at Antioch"** Acts 11:26

Today we get the blessing of looking at two different and distinct titles that have been attributed to believers for centuries. The first is "disciple" and the second is "Christian".

A "disciple" is a pupil, plain and simple. It is not complicated and it is not meant to illicit a hierarchy in any way shape or form. Every person born on the planet will be taught how to live life. You will learn the easy way through being taught, or you will learn the hard way through the school of hard knocks. In some areas you may be more open to learning through somebody teaching you, and in other areas you will have to learn through experience.

Life is so much easier when you are teachable. God expresses very clearly in His Word that we need spiritual leaders who will lovingly parent us into the truths of God. If you cannot humble yourself to learn from someone who only desires to help you grow, you hinder your own growth and the opportunity to be blessed. Jesus expects all believers to be discipled and to have a teachable heart so they can follow His way of living. Our highest goal should be to be like Him.

Acts 11:26 says that the "disciples" were first called Christians in the city of Antioch. The term Christian is a 2000 year old term. It did not start out as a term of endearment. Instead, the term was meant to illicit shame by mocking the One who had been cursed, ridiculed, charged as a criminal and who died a criminal's death by being crucified. The fact that the name has stuck for 2000 years has great meaning, as it implies that the Christians respected the title. To be a Christian meant that you were a "little Christ". You acted like Him, talked like Him, loved like Him and clearly represented Him to the world. Following Him as He has called us to do requires that we represent His nature and personhood in a clear and untainted way.

There are no lone rangers in the kingdom of God. We all need help to be all that God intended us to be. You cannot be a Christian unless you are first a disciple. Disciples are those who have opened their hearts to be trained and to be taught.

They are willing to be transparent and they are willing to learn. They do not have an attitude that says, “I can do this all by myself and I can figure it out all on my own.” No natural child starts life with this attitude and, if they did, they would learn very quickly and painfully that life does not work that way.

The spiritual principle, “first the natural and then the spiritual” most certainly applies here (1 Corinthians 15:46). Just as natural children need natural teachers to teach them the ways of life, so spiritual children need spiritual teachers to teach them the ways of the Kingdom. When they are taught properly, they will mature to a place where the name Christian can also be applied, for they will have learned how to be “like Christ” and be deserving of the title “Christian”.

*Lord God, open my eyes to see those You have placed in my life to assist me in my journey of being more like You. I am willing to be a student of Your truths, to be taught by You and by my fellow brothers and sisters. Thank you for the vision of one day being more and more like You.*

## Day 7

## Co-Labourers

**"You could not possibly do such a thing: to kill the righteous with the wicked, treating the righteous and the wicked alike. You could not possibly do that! Won`t the Judge of all the earth do what is just?"** Genesis 18:25

My pastor has told the story numerous times of how, before he came to Christ, he had very low self-esteem. But after he came to Christ and began walking with the Lord, it began to dawn on him: *Hey, God really, really loves me and He needs me because He has limited Himself to use man as His ambassadors. He needs me to extend His kingdom in the earth. He doesn't have to use me—He could find other ways—but He has chosen me to be a vessel and an instrument for His own happiness. That means I am important. That means I am special.* And with that truth firmly embedded in his spirit, low self-esteem had met its match.

The God of Heaven has limited Himself to use human instruments to accomplish His lofty purposes. I was awestruck at the idea of being called and chosen by God to be His very own son. And then to think that His Holy Spirit would take up residence inside of me, that He longs to hear my prayers and to spend time with me. Psalm 139 says, "...such knowledge is too wonderful for me..." and Psalm 8 says, "What is man that you are even mindful of him?" Yet, He is so much more than mindful of us, for His heart and mind are overwhelmed with grandiose plans and purposes for us (see also Jeremiah 29:11).

God, from the very beginning of time, has used men and women to accomplish His will and His purposes. He says in Ezekiel 22:30, "He sought for a man to stand in the gap of intercessory prayer, but he could not find one." God's eyes run to and fro throughout the whole earth looking for hearts that are committed and dedicated to Him so that He might call them into co-laboring service with Him.

God had given Adam and Eve assignments and in the evening God came to commune with them. Adam would have explained, "These are the creatures I named today: the Lion, the Tiger, the Leopard, and the Cheetah. What wondrous creatures You have made, and here is why I named them what I named them." We see a picture of Adam and Eve walking with God at the end of the day going over the details of the assignments they had given to them.

Genesis 18 is the perfect example of the kind of friendship that God wants to have with us. Abraham was called the friend of God. Abraham communed with God, "I get it that Sodom and Gomorrah are wretched, but You are perfect and holy and You can only give righteous judgment. If there are some righteous folk down there, You can't just obliterate them as well!" Wow, what a relationship that Abraham enjoyed with God! God brought Him into that place of honor and prestige to allow Him to intercede on behalf of Sodom and Gomorrah.

God brings us into that place as well, as we pray for our cities and share our faith and pray for the sick and release people from bondages. Jesus commissioned 82 people to go out and minister to cities before He went and visited them. He sent "the seventy", as they are called, as well as the 12 disciples—each with the same mission and purpose of God—to preach, "Repent for the Kingdom of God is at hand." Then Jesus would come into the city and hearts would be opened and transformations would take place. We are God's co-laborers today to minister His love.

*Lord Jesus, YOU were declared a friend of sinners, prostitutes, tax collector's, Samaritans and other less desirables. Your very disciples were made up of something very interesting characters. Your heart was that the lost be found, you befriended all who came to you. Let Your Spirit of love and acceptance overflow me that I would display YOUR love, Your acceptance to a lost and dying world.*

## Month One

## The Believer's Identity

### Week One

1. In the past week of reading, which devotional stood out the most too you and why?
2. Religion teaches us to fear God, but Jesus came to reveal God as a loving intimate Father, in your heart of hearts is this how you are interacting with God? If not what truth do you need to revisit so that you can live in this relationship with God?
3. If God sees you as the "righteousness of God in Christ" what does that communicate to your life, is it that God Accepts You, Does it give you a sense of Security, or does it speak to your significance?
4. If Jesus was willing to be the Father's love slave, what should we desire to be and what will indicate its accomplishment?
5. Pick one Verse to memorize from this past week of scriptures.

## Day 8

## I am a Friend of God

**You are my friends when you do the things I command you. I'm no longer calling you servants because servants don't understand what their master is thinking and planning. No, I've named you friends because I've let you in on everything I've heard from the Father.** John 15:5

You and I are "companions with the Holy Spirit". Now that is a beautiful thought. There are numerous truths in the Word of God about who we are and about how men and women of God knew Him so intimately.

- Abraham is called the "friend of God" (James 2:23).
- Moses knew God "face to face" – closer than a friend (Exodus 33:11).
- David is called "a man after God's own heart" (Acts 13:22).
- Jeremiah is said to be the "weeping prophet" whose heart was broken with the things that broke God's heart. (Lamentations 1:16, 2:11)

The list could go on illustrating the unique relationship God offers us. Today, we will briefly look at the glorious connection between the believer and the Holy Spirit. These are the days of God's heart, what He always desired for mankind. God desires to be on the inside of us so that He can shine out through us but also, more importantly so He can have a divine intimate communion with us. With the Holy Spirit living in us, we have this "treasure in an earthen vessel" (2 Corinthians 4:7).

The writer of Hebrews describes our connection to the Holy Spirit as though we were companions with Him. Here is "Dictionary.com's" definition of a companion

**com·pan·ion**

- a person who is frequently in the company of, associates with, or accompanies another
- Person employed to accompany, assist, or live with another in the capacity of a helpful friend.
- A mate or match for something

We have the opportunity to be called a companion of the Holy Spirit. The verse is quick to iterate that all of this wonder and glory can be presumed upon and lost entirely to the new believer. But for the believer who holds on to the engrafted seed and commits to Christ all that they are, than the Holy Spirit is your companion. The greatest revivalists of all time had a deep intimate personal relationship with the Holy Spirit. God on the inside is the greatest news we could ever have, for now our comforter, our strength and helper lives in us and enables us to achieve the very will and purpose of God. (Colossians 1:27)

Companionship is a two way relationship. You cannot have one person willing to give everything to the relationship while the other person is only half-hearted. Relationships become great because of the greatness of the commitment from both parties. The same can be said of any great marriage. It was never carried on the back of just one of the participants. The commitment of both individuals to deepen the relationship and pay the price to go to the next level is what makes the relationship strong and enables it to weather the storms of life.

The Holy Spirit is more than willing. He left heaven to take up residence inside of us. He is committed all the way to the end of time. He lifts us up, strengthens us, encourages us and heals us.

What do we bring to the table? How are we helpful? And yet, God calls us friends.

*My God, My all, I can only bring myself to you, without you I can do nothing, can profit nothing, can produce nothing, but with YOU working in me and through me the potential is limitless. To contemplate that you partner with me and call me Friend and Companion causes my heart to overflow with praise and joy. At the end of my days let it be said of me what it was said of Abraham, that I too as a friend of God.*

## Day 9

### Worshippers

**"But an hour is coming, and is now here, when the true worshipers will worship the Father in spirit and truth. Yes, the Father wants such people to worship Him. [24] God is spirit, and those who worship Him must worship in spirit and truth."** John 4:23

Man was created to worship God. Worship is central to who we are and what we do. It would not be an understatement to declare that man actually longs for something to worship. We are constantly searching for something or someone worthy of our worship, adoration and love. We allow many things to try and fill that void, whether it is idols, ideologies, religion, success, fame, family, relationships (moral or immoral), riches, politics, the arts or ourselves. Mankind has always found something to worship.

The truth is, however, that we were created by God to worship *Him*. We find the greatest fulfillment in life through loving and knowing Him. No encounter with God has ever left a person the same and, because of the revelation of God that they have experienced, their worship is never the same. Abraham, Jacob, Moses, Joshua, Job, Isaiah, Daniel and Ezekiel have all stood in the very presence of God and were radically transformed.

Worship is what happens in our heart when we receive a revelation of God. It is impossible to have a revelation of God and not respond in worship. The simplest of translations of the word worship is to bow, to knell or to prostrate oneself 1. Because of the powerful, awe inspiring, glorious, supernatural presence of God, the wicked heart would seek either to escape or to respond in brokenness and repentance. But for those of us who have the privilege of knowing Him, the greater His presence, the greater our worship will be. Revelation equals worship and when we worship with all our hearts as a lifestyle, more revelation of God will come into our lives. If we continue to live worshipfully, the process will continue and we will be transformed into His likeness.

When I had a salvation encounter with God, I was overwhelmed with the knowledge of His love for me. It caused me to spend nights and mornings in songs of praise to Him. All I wanted to do was worship and praise God, although at the time I did not know the name of what I was doing.

Truly converted people will be worshippers. They will be so filled with gratitude, thanksgiving and praise that it will be like a river of water flowing out of their heart to God. When the children were told by the Pharisees to stop praising Jesus, He said, "If they kept quiet, the stones would do it for them, shouting praise" (Luke 19:40).

God the Father is looking for worshippers. You cannot know God and not worship Him. It's not out of duty or obedience, but out of love, adoration and thanksgiving. If we cannot be grateful for the cross of Jesus Christ, then there is nothing left for God to do on our behalf to cause us to praise and worship Him. The cross should seal our worship attitude forever and ever and ever and ever.

*Take some time right now and lift up your voice and your hands and begin to worship God for who He is: faithful, loving, forgiving, gracious and powerful.*

*1 Strong's Exhaustive Concordance, Hebrew word shawkhaw #7812; published in 1890 – Public Domain*

## Day 10

## The Bride of Christ

**"This mystery is profound, but I am talking about Christ and the church. To sum up, each one of you is to love his wife as himself, and the wife is to respect her husband."** Ephesians 5: 32-33

Our relationship with God for eternity is initiated with what is called "the marriage supper of the Lamb". The apostle Paul speaks of engaging us to Christ as a pure undefiled virgin. The marriage union is the most intimate, transparent, giving and rewarding relationship for a man and a woman to have on earth. It is the great gift from God to mankind. Bishop Joseph Garlington made the statement, "The purpose of marriage is not to make us happy, but instead to make us holy." 2 When we understand that, we will above all people be most contented.

It should not take us by surprise that our relationship with our Saviour is likened to a marriage. The aspect that I want to focus on today is that of intimate communication. God is not a God of the mind, but of the heart. He is not a God focused on our performance alone, but a God who judges our motives and intents.

God in all His "OMNI-Realities"—Omnipresent, Omniscience, Omnipotent—does not need anything from us. And yet, He has chosen to invite and enlist us in overseeing earth. Man, who is made from earth and named after earth (Adam means "ruddy, earthy"), is called by God to administrate the earth from whence he came. It is also a prophetic picture that before a man can rule in godly authority, he must have control of himself—what the Bible calls "self-control". We do this through our prayer life with God.

Prayer is communication. It is both speaking and being spoken to. It was never intended to be a one-way dialogue. God speaks through various means to us, so we need to have "ears to hear what the Spirit is saying to the churches" (Revelations 2:7, 11, 17, 29; 3:6, 13). Jesus repeatedly said in His ministry, "He who has ears, let him hear" (Matthew 11:15; Mark 4:9; Luke 14:35).

God is a communicator; all of creation is declaring the glory of God (Psalm 19:1). When we come to God and commune with Him from our heart, He hears and He speaks and He answers.

Be comfortable in prayer. Never say you don't know how to pray, for prayer is not a performance. There is no wrong way to be honest other than to not believe that God will hear and will answer. It is much more our heart that God is listening to than our words alone. We need to remove ourselves from the formula-centered idea of prayer and come to the heart-centered prayer of Scripture. God responds to our heart's cry—we need not be afraid to voice our inmost desires. The wonderful grace of marriage is that we can share our hearts with each other and find total acceptance and understanding. We dare not think God would do less. He does so much more!

*Take time to pray from your heart. What do you want to express to the Lord about growing in intimate relationship with Him?*

2 Garlington, J. (1995, March). "Marriage" Sermon presented City Bible Church, Portland, Oregon

## Day 11

### I am God's Ambassador

**Therefore, we are ambassadors for Christ; certain that God is appealing through us, we plead on Christ's behalf, "Be reconciled to God."** 2 Corinthians 5:20

Let's just take a minute and consider what some of the benefits are of being an ambassador. Some key benefits are as follows.

- Living in a foreign land.
- An Ambassadors national Army protects them while abroad.
- A direct line to the highest political office in their home country.
- An Ambassador is protected from legal prosecution while abroad.
- Represents the interests, desires and heartbeat of another kingdom.

The Word of God says that you are Jesus' ambassador in the earth. That means you have taken up residence in another country. You have a "passport" to be here to do a work for God. The Bible teaches us that we are in enemy territory, (1 Corinthians 4:4; John 4:4.) This means that we have protectors, bodyguards who look after you who are unseen but very present. These bodyguards are called "guardian angels" but they don't wear red berets.

Because you are a representative of another country working for a higher cause, there will be times when opposition to God's plans is severe. Right then, you need to know that you have a direct line to God's heart. You must always remember that nothing can happen to you on earth that is not authorized from above. As you submit your life to the God of the universe and as you live under His grace and by His spirit, God will supersede the natural laws of this planet to help you and to bless you. (2 Kings 6:17).

The last and best point of all is that God is making His appeal through you and me, for those who do not know Him to come back to Him. He is calling them by name. He is seeking their face at His table. Oh how He loves them and desires they come and feast with Him (Revelations 2:20). He paid such a wondrous price when He bled and died for the whole world. He calls through us for them to come back to Him, to come back to their true home. As an ambassador, you are working for eternal purposes, enabling those who do not know Christ to have the opportunity to be saved (2 Corinthians 5:16-21).

You are a representative of another kingdom. You may not look like it and you may not feel like it, but it is true because you have a living powerful relationship with the God of the universe. What sets you and I apart is that we are called to be a people of His presence. Moses declared that the entire nation of Israel would not take one step forward without the very presence of God leading them and guiding them because the only thing that separated Israel from any other nation was the presence of God (Exodus 33: 1-16). We are marked and uniquely different not because of our education, finances, good looks or perfume, but because of God's Spirit abiding in us and causing those who are outside the Kingdom to be drawn into the Kingdom. You are marked, you are sealed, you are different because God's Spirit indwells you and makes you His representative.

*Daddy, as I open my eyes each morning, I observe around me that many people have no concept of Your great love. I am learning each day more of who I am in You. I now see that I am to be an ambassador for Your Kingdom in my everyday life. Help me to do this. I am not sure how to do it, when to do it or with whom to do it, but I trust You to show me the way, in Jesus name.*

## Day 12

### I am a Royal Priest

**But you are a chosen race, a royal priesthood, a holy nation, a people for His possession, so that you may proclaim the praises of the One who called you out of darkness into His marvelous light. "**1 Peter 2:9

Previously, we looked at the truth of our being heirs of God's Kingdom. The fact that He is a King makes us princes and princesses. The Bible clearly states our kingship and describes the process God uses to train us for the day that we will reign and rule with Him. We are royalty, created to express God's kingly authority in the earth.

We are not just royalty, however. The Bible also says that we are priests. Part of our purpose on the earth, therefore, is to train others in godliness. We have looked at being ambassadors and sharing God's heart, but when people respond to God's invitation, we are then called to train and teach them how to live lives that are filled with the evidence of a true conversion.

One of the key responsibilities of a priest or minister is to present sacrifices that are acceptable to God. The bible as you will find is a gold mine and like gold there can be much found on the surface, but to really hit pay dirt or what was once termed the mother load, you must dig and dig and dig. The Bible is similar and when we read the Old Testament we learn that God was preparing us for the New Testament. There are numerous prophetic prophesies that are fulfilled in the life of Jesus in the New Testament. Along with the literal prophetic promises fulfilled in the New Testament there are a myriad of truths hidden as pictures and photographs that find their true purpose and meaning in the life of a New Testament believer, you and I. We call these things Types and Shadows because the ultimate fulfillment of it was not what the Old Testament individual experienced but foretold what we would experience. For instance, there were numerous Old Testament sacrifices that were types and shadows that we are meant to fulfill. All of the sacrifices served as a constant reminder to the worshipper of how costly his sin was, is or could be. The priest offered up sacrifices that God accepted in preparation of His Son's coming and dying in our place. Though the covenant has changed, our priestly purpose has changed very little: we worship, bring the sacrifice of praise, intercede, fast and live worthy lives so that we might draw the unsaved into relationship with God. (1Corinthians 10:1-11; John 3:14,15)

Our prayers become prayers of intercession. Simply put, intercession is selflessly praying for those who do not know God to come to know God. Our highest priestly duty is fulfilled in both worship and prayer that is centered on God's love flowing out through us to those who do not know Him.

God will put people on your heart to pray for and you will find yourself wanting to tell others about Jesus and what He has done for you. It's only natural, for you are a priest of the highest God. You may never go to Bible school or seminary, but that will never take away from the reality of your call to the priesthood.

**Isaiah 61:6a And you will be called priests of the Lord, you will be named ministers of our God.**

*Daddy, I thank you for my call to service to You and to the world around me. It is exhilarating to be called a priest of God and to know that is part of why I am here. I do not want to hold this joy and excitement on the inside. I want to tell others about You, so I ask You to cause me to overflow with Your love and grace. I choose to tell others about You. I know you will make me successful in being a witness for You.*

## Day 13

### Surpassing Glory

**For if the ministry of condemnation had glory, the ministry of righteousness overflows with even more glory. [10] In fact, what had been glorious is not glorious now by comparison because of the glory that surpasses it.[11] For if what was fading away was glorious, what endures will be even more glorious.** 2 Corinthians 3:9-11

What is the benefit to having God living on the inside? Was it not sufficient to have the Holy Spirit overshadowing the prophets, priests and kings? The New Testament economy is significantly different from the Old Testament economy. We cannot fully recognize the benefits of God living in the inside until we come to terms with what the expectation or the standard upon the New Testament believer is in comparison to that of the Old Testament believer.

I am not just referring to Israel under Moses or the Law, but to the entire Old Testament economy of faith. Great visitations, phenomenal miracles, glorious signs and wonders, covenants that blessed God's people—none of these compare with what is to be the norm for those who have been filled and baptized with the Holy Spirit.

Jesus' entire ministry was operating in the Old Testament. Though we start our New Testament at the beginning of the book of Matthew, God does not start the New Testament era until Matthew 27, Mark 15, Luke 22 and John 19, when Jesus is crucified and His blood ratifies the New Covenant. Before that, Jesus is functioning under the promise of the Old Covenants of the Messiah, who would come and be the suffering servant, the branch, the prophet greater than Moses and on and on we could go.

Jesus came to usher in a new era of revelation and relationship between God and man that could not be accomplished under the Old Covenants. This New Covenant in His blood changed everything: a torn veil, no sacrifices, new laws (the greatest of which is love), God indwelling, unity of God's children, Holy Spirit power for every believer, greater promises and a greater call to the miraculous. Jesus said, "Greater things than I do, you shall do because I go to the Father" (John 14:12).

In the church where I got saved, I was taught against modern day baptism in the Holy Spirit and that demonic oppression was a thing of the past. I hungered for God's word. It was my daily bread. I attended four churches, three of which were "Spirit filled". During a drive back from Florida assisting a ministry team, I was baptized in the Holy Spirit. Though my relationship with God had been exemplary and powerful and intimate, a whole new dimension opened to me. Before I even knew what prophecy was, I would prophecy future events in the Church and into my life. The reality of a God who was alive and did miracles became normal for me as I began seeing God use ministries to bring healing and deliverance to people's lives. This is New Testament Christianity—Knowing Jesus, the Lover of our souls; seeing the needy, the broken, the lame, the discouraged and the blind made whole. He calls us to do what He would do—ministering life, health and healing and bringing God-desired change right into their very existence.

- I am a carrier of the presence of Almighty God.
- Signs, wonders and miracles are my inheritance to reveal God and save souls.
- Because God is in me, I am the devils worst nightmare, just like Jesus was.
- Victorious, overcoming, glorious living is the mandate for the price has been paid.
- All the promises of God are YES and AMEN.

*Daddy, it is so wonderful to consider how much You desire that I live in Your presence. Your passionate love extends to those who do not yet know You. The feast has been prepared and by Your Spirit's empowerment we draw people to Your love. Move us out of the natural and into the supernatural, for all Your saints let the supernatural become our natural for that is Your dwelling place.*

## Day 14

## Makeover Specialists

**"You'll use the old rubble of past lives to build a new, rebuild the foundations from out of your past. You'll be known as those who can fix anything, restore old ruins, rebuild and renovate, make the community liveable again."** Isaiah 58:12(The Message)

**"They'll rebuild the old ruins; raise a new city out of the wreckage. They'll start over on the ruined cities, take the rubble left behind and make it new."** Isaiah 61:4 (The Message)

Are you good with a hammer? Not to worry, I am not that great with a hammer either. If you need something fixed the person to call would by either my brother or my brother in law

God loves to fix broken things. We have all seen the makeover shows and how transformed a house can be when they are finished with the procedure. Well, I have a funny feeling that God can do it better than anybody. The anointing we spoke of yesterday on Jesus is first mentioned in Isaiah 61. Verse 4 outlines the results of an anointed life, similar to what is recorded in Isaiah 58 which is the result of people who have truly discovered the lifestyle most pleasing to God.

God loves to holler for the underdog, the one that no one expects to achieve anything, the poor that no one expects could ever win in life. The rejected, the abused, the broken hearted–God loves to come and revive them to a fullness they have never ever experienced (Isaiah 57:15; 1 Samuel 2:8). If God is in the business of restoring lives, He thinks we should do it as well, because He is with us (John 14:12). World missions are a living testimony to all who will look at the results honestly and without bias. It is a testimony of how people and nations can come into the destiny God always intended.

History is indeed His Story of how grace interacts with humanity and produces greatness. Both Old and New Testaments are examples of how God restores and revives lives from sadness to joy, from poverty to riches, from slavery to freedom and from barrenness to fruitfulness. Now God partners with us and says this is a "Family Enterprise". We are Holy Ghost incorporated to go and heal families, organizations and governments.

Should we be afraid of the challenges set before us or should we by faith bring the fullness of His Kingdom to those around us by His Spirit's power (Hebrews 11:1; John 5:4-5)?

*Lord, I am personally challenged to think that You have called me to help repair a broken and fallen world. I offer myself to You and ask You by Your Spirit to enable me to use the influence You will give me to lift up the person of Jesus to the world around me. I dare to believe that You will work miracles through me as I follow your Spirit's direction.*

## Week Two

1. From Day 6 where we learned about being a Disciple, what does the word literally mean and why should we want to be discipled?
2. Does prayer ever feel like a performance, what should it be like? If we are rating our prayers and others prayers what exactly does that say about our relationship with God?
3. What should seal our "worship attitude forever and ever and ever"?
4. Quote your verce from last week and now pick a new one.

## Day 15

### Salty Seasoning

**"Let me tell you why you are here. You're here to be salt-seasoning that brings out the God-flavors of this earth. If you lose your saltiness, how will people taste godliness? You've lost your usefulness and will end up in the garbage.** Matthew 5:13 (The Message)

I don't know about you, but one of the joys of my life is sitting down to a good meal. I have been ever so blessed to marry an Italian wife who could easily be a chef. She learned from both her father and her mother how to cook perfectly. Having travelled to a number of different countries for both short and long periods of time, I have a very wide appreciation for food. One thing holds true: seasoning can turn something bland into a flavourful delicacy.

No doubt, Jesus Himself had this in mind when He said to His disciples, "Fella's, hey get this! You are like salt, and you are here to influence and accentuate life to the fullest. You are to show the world how they were truly meant to live from the beginning. Your saltiness/influence will enable people to taste and see that God is good. Without your saltiness/influence, the world has no way of really seeing Me for who I am."

There is a story of little boy who was quite sad and had a string of very difficult circumstances. He was encouraged to go and pray and give it to Jesus and everything would be all right. The little boy's reply was quite poignant: "Right now I need a Jesus with skin on". That is God's feeling exactly and that is why He came. The world needed a God with skin on. So God put on skin and we know Him as the Son of God, Jesus.

What made Jesus so unique was HIS CHARACTER, the common people loved him, the religious leaders hated Him. Both of them were looking for a different type of Messiah. They never expected a loving, caring, compassionate, just and liberating Messiah. They wanted another King David; they did not expect a suffering servant who carried our sins. His influence was so felt that nobody having met him or hearing him was not impacted by who He is. He was God with skin on, hidden from our view by flesh but open to our eyes if we would look with our hearts. Without our saltiness/influence, Jesus tells us that He has no more need of us and we will be thrown in the garbage. Would you keep salt in your cupboard if it no longer had any flavour? I don't think so. You would not keep something worthless in your cupboard; you would get rid of it. That is how God feels about Christians who have the title, the theology and the terminology but have no power, influence or ability to make the lost thirsty for what we have.

A restaurant stays open when it serves food that people can't wait to have. A restaurant will close if it serves bland, ordinary, run-of-the mill food. Who is going to pay good money for that? No one. “Word of mouth" will keep a restaurant in business for a very long time. People talk and talk about the great food and atmosphere at the restaurant.

Christians should have "word of mouth" testimonies of who He is in their lives. We just can't stop talking about Him. We have a God-ordained purpose to influence the world toward godliness and toward God Himself. Our lifestyles speak so loudly and clearly of a God with skin on, that people will be drawn to our testimony. Count me in!

What about you? Are you willing to take the plunge and not be ashamed of the greatest message the world will ever hear? God is looking for those servants who will boldly live in such a way that Jesus is clearly communicated through them to the world around them.

*Daddy, thank You for making my life an influence when I am not even aware of it. I desire to be living testimony of who You are and to have an attitude that gladly, respectfully and powerfully reveals You to others so they can have the fullness of joy You desire for them.*

## Day 16

## Light of Truth

**"Here's another way to put it: You're here to be light, bringing out the God-colors in the world. God is not a secret to be kept. We're going public with this, as public as a city on a hill. If I make you light-bearers, you don't think I'm going to hide you under a bucket, do you? I'm putting you on a light stand. Now that I've put you there on a hilltop, on a light stand—shine! Keep open house; be generous with your lives. By opening up to others, you'll prompt people to open up with God, this generous Father in heaven."** Matthew 5:14-16 (The Message)

The city of Jerusalem is set on seven hills. I have been blessed to travel to Israel. Upon landing just outside Jerusalem, we were bused into the great city. It was dark when we left Jericho and, as we rounded one last bend, we saw the lights of Jerusalem. It is truly a city set on a hill that simply cannot be hid.

The believer, the Church, is a city on a hill. We are light revealing the glory and the perfection of God. It is important to understand that God has no desire whatsoever to hide us. Instead He wants to place us in the most beneficial spot possible. When you design a house, the lights are never put in obscure places. No, they are front and center so that they can be a  benefit for everyone. . You don't hide light; you use it to bless everybody.

We could go into the scientific characteristics of light but we will not take the time to do so. However, we all understand that without light and the warmth that it brings, we would be a lifeless planet. So our significance is without question. We should be filled with an inner confidence and excitement that comes from knowing we are integral to God's plan.

One key characteristic of light is that it dispels darkness. Both light and darkness cannot dwell in the same place at the same time. The truth of the good news of Jesus Christ will dispel the darkness of the enemy in people's lives. The Bible clearly states that, for this purpose, the Son of God was manifest to destroy the works of the evil one (1 John 3:8). The more light is proclaimed, the more darkness will be dispelled.

Light is also a personification of truth. Where there is truth, lies cannot remain. Satan is the father of lies and uses deception to ensnare people's lives. As long as a person's faith is put in a lie, that lie has power over a person's life. When truth or light comes in, the lies of the darkness are dispelled. Jesus promised us that truth would set us free entirely and completely (John 8:32). In so many ways, the battles we fight are "truth wars"—when we believe the truth, the war is over. God calls us to proclaim the truth of His ways to those who do not know Him and bring them into light of His glorious Kingdom.

*Lord, I accept that part of Your ultimate plan and purpose is to put Your children in a place of prominence so that Your glory may be revealed to a world that is in utter darkness. Though You may allow seasons of obscurity, You will, in your perfect wisdom, use our lives to reveal Your love and power. Thank You that I will be used by You to touch other lives.*

## Day 17

### A Fisherman

**"Follow Me, he told them, and I will make you fish for people!"** Matthew 4:19

Everything that man has ever made was made for a purpose. Almost nothing created was created indiscriminately. In other words a need, a want or a desire came first and then, to fulfill a purpose, a stapler, a car, a plane, an eraser, or whatever it is was invented.

From God's perspective, we are no different. Although God needs nothing and did not create us out of necessity, He hotwired us to live for meaning and purpose. We wither without a purpose. We are driven to answer the questions "Why?" and "What for?" and "What will happen next?" and the infamous "Are we there yet?" God designed us and made us for every one of the identities that we have look at so far in this book. It is not a list you can ignore for each one is a unique revelation of who we are and what we do.

One day, Peter fished all night with his brothers and workers and came up empty handed. The Lord commanded him to let down the net on the other side. Peter wisely obeyed Christ's command although it went against all common sense. Peter hauled in a mother lode of fish and was overwhelmed with the reality of the blessing and the means.

Peter was then convicted of his worthlessness and of Christ's worthiness and said to Jesus, "Depart from me for I am a sinful man." In view of his humility and brokenness, Christ responded, "From now on, you will be fishing for men."

It's quite a concept but that is the purpose for which Christ came—to seek and to save that which was lost. Jesus selected 12 men that we call Apostles; they were given the initial responsibility of taking the good news about Christ to the world. Jesus did not limit this call or responsibility to leadership in the Church, every believer has the ministry of reconciliation. To truly be like Jesus we must have His heart for those who have not yet come to His saving grace.

What does it really mean to be like Jesus? What comes to your mind when that question is asked? Is it His patience during suffering, His vision to fulfill the plan of salvation, reproducing His ministry of healing and miracle? Or is it being able to speak with such wisdom that others are dumbfounded by our eloquence, not one of these is the primary issue of Jesus life or example, He came for one purpose, to bring us back to the Father. He came that we might know and receive His great love and to invite others to receive it as well. Are we like Jesus in that capacity? Are we driven to the point of willingness to lay down our own lives that another person might come into the Kingdom? If we want to truly have the heart of God, it will be a heart that seeks to draw people from their darkness to the light of Christ.

Jesus made a promise to all of us: “Follow Me and I will make you fishers of men”. We continually quote the promise "I will build My church and the gates of hell will not prevail against it" but we forget that the two promises are connected. Gates are protective; they guard against attack. The church, having followed Jesus to rescue sinners, is breaking down the gates of hell to rescue the lost and dying. Sometimes I think a better translation of Christ's intent would be, “I will build My Church to attack the gates of hell and they will crumble.” To be His Church, His Bride, His equal, we must be like *Him* and He is still inviting all to His banqueting table.

*Daddy, I join with Your heart to be a fisher of people, to launch out into the depths of humanity to find those that You are drawing to Yourself. I want to be like You in Your love for those who do not know who You are. Help me to reveal You in purity and truth. I am assured that as I follow YOU, YOU will make me one who fishes for people. The true test of your leading will be that it guides me to love others and draw them to YOU.*

## Day 18

## Soldiers in Service

**``Put on the full armor of God so that you can stand against the tactics of the Devil``** Ephesians 6:11

There can be much misunderstanding when people who do not know the Lord hear believers use military terminology. Historically, those who have called themselves Christians have blighted the name of Christ by killing in His name, something He never authorised them to do. As a matter of fact, Jesus made it very clear that those who live by the sword would die by the sword (Luke22:38, Matt.26:52).

War was not and is not God's plan for His Church. And yet, half of the Bible is filled with wars and with men of God who are likened to modern day generals, army strategists and presidents. The majority of these men of God in the Old Testament engaged in some manner of actual literal warfare. In the New Testament the warfare is not natural but spiritual, our enemies are not flesh and blood but demonic and devilish. When we go back to the beginning—right back to the garden—and we hear God's original mandate for man, we see that God called Adam and Eve and their offspring to have dominion, to populate the earth and to subdue it. Two of these words have military connotations, which make this a very profound statement, for who else was in the garden for them to conquer and dominate?

The two key words are as follows:

Dominion - H7287 -rawdaw

A primitive root; to *tread* down, that is, *subjugate*; specifically to *crumble* off: - (come to, make to) have dominion, prevail against, reign, (bear, make to) rule, (-r, over), take. 3

Subdue - H3533 kabash

A primitive root; to *tread* down; hence negatively to *disregard*; positively to *conquer, subjugate, violate:* - bring into bondage, force, keep under, subdue, bring into subjection. 4

Mankind, like his Maker, was to rule and reign in life. We were intended to be princes and princesses on our way to a throne and a kingdom. From the very beginning of human history, God has put in our DNA the desire to overcome, lead, prevail, reign, conquer, subjugate, bring into bondage and forcibly rule. Unfortunately, we can look at human history and see how man has made the gruesome horrible mistake of doing this to each other instead of to the intended thief from the garden.

Our battle is not natural but spiritual and the weapons are mighty through God to the pulling down of the spiritual strongholds intended to keep us from our destiny of ruling and reigning with Christ. In other words, the enemy that we are meant to rule over is Satan and his demonic cohorts. God never intended we take scriptures about warfare and use them to wage war on one another. When we see the real enemy behind the scenes pulling the strings of man, we are to cut off his power and bring him under subjection to the will of God.

Our mindset is the greatest battleground of all. We cannot, as the scripture so clearly indicates, be enlisted and yet live as a civilian. My dad was in the Canadian army. I was born on an army base and grew up on army bases throughout Germany. Army life and civilian life are very different. In order for us to be mature overcomers, we must understand first and foremost that we are enlisted in God's army, an army whose purpose is to win the lost and extend God's Kingdom.

*I accept my enlistment, Father. I submit to training and I prepare for war. Thank you that the victory is already assured.*

*3 Strong, James, Strong's Exhaustive Concordance of the Bible, (1890) Forty Eighth Edition Hebrew Dictionary 7287*

*4 Strong, James, Strong's Exhaustive Concordance of the Bible, (1890) Forty Eight Edition Hebrew Dictionary 3533*

## Day 19

## Warriors

**A final word: Be strong in the Lord and in his mighty power. Put on all of God's armor so that you will be able to stand firm against all strategies of the devil. For we[c] are not fighting against flesh-and-blood enemies, but against evil rulers and authorities of the unseen world, against mighty powers in this dark world, and against evil spirits in the heavenly places.** Ephesians 6:10-12

The Word of God starts out with a very simple statement: "In the beginning, God". The spiritual realm existed before the natural realm. We cannot escape the absoluteness of the spiritual realm that houses both angels and demons. God says to you and to me, "You have an enemy, a real enemy that is not flesh and blood, not like anything you have fought before. Get ready." The Scripture before us is not meant to alarm us but to prepare us.

How great is it to have a Saviour who did not send us to do something in which He did not already lead the way! ***Heb. 4:15 This High Priest of ours understands our weaknesses, for he faced all of the same testing's we do, yet he did not sin.*** Jesus' ministry was not started until He went into the wilderness and was tempted by the enemy, yet He did not falter. The story of Scripture is an overwhelming affirmation that servants of God can and will defeat their enemies because God is with them. ***For this purpose was the Son of God manifest to destroy the works of the evil one. 1 John 4:8c)***

The corroboration of history since Scripture was written is that God is a God who enables His children to defeat Satan's hold on nations and turn them back to God. George Whitfield, Smith Wigglesworth, John and Charles Wesley–revivalists all—show us that the day of defeating the works of darkness are before us not behind us. As formidable a foe as the enemy is, God is fighting through us. It is His battle and He has already won it for us.

God tells us, "I have a full cache of weapons for you that are proven for you in the battle you are about to face." Therefore, when we are fully armoured, we are able to stand and to withstand all that hell will throw at us. But here is the greatest news: When we choose to turn the tables and, under Christ's command, assault the enemy's fortress, it will fall. **Matthew 16:18c I will build My church, and the gates of hell shall not prevail against it.**

As a new Christian reading the Word of God, I was always enamored by the battles of the Old Testament—especially the exploits of David and his mighty men. We know from the New Testament that our battle is not physical but spiritual. However, we in the New Testament must have the same attitude of a warrior that the Old Testament men of God had. This is one of the reasons why the record of their lives has been left for us. We are warriors of the King and we are assured of victory as we follow the examples set before us.

*Lord God of Armies, as You have been declared so many times in Your Word, I may not have understood it when I first accepted You, but I am enlisted in Your army. I will familiarize myself with the weapons You have provided for me, so that I might be able to stand against all that hell would throw against me. How awesome to know that "greater is He that is in me than he that is in the world" and that You constantly lead me into victory (1 John 4:4; 2 Corinthians 2:14).*

## Day 20

### Loving Intercessor

**"And we have come to know and to believe the love that God has for us. God is love, and the one who remains in love remains in God, and God remains in him."** 1 John 4:16

*Father, thank You for the last 19 days of truth that has ministered to our hearts. Thank You for grace that has been poured into the lives of your sons and your daughters as they have made a commitment to set apart time each day to minister to You. As we end this month, I pray for the moving of Your Holy Spirit in their lives in a greater distinction.*

*Your Word declares that You are the God who is love, not the God who has love but the God who is love. I pray in the mighty name of Jesus that each son and daughter who has read through this devotional would be overflowing with the power of Your love and be ambassadors of Your love. I pray that they would know that, first and foremost, the desire of Your heart is that they would know You in the height and depth and width and breadth of your love. Lord, I pray that, as people meet them, they would know that they're Christians because of Your love inside of them that flows out of them. I pray that they would be a people of compassion, a people of mercy, a people of grace. Lord, help them to be like Paul who was compelled to give to others and to show love to them.*

*Daddy, I pray that they would be God pleasers that they would not be man pleasers. What would dominate inside of their heart in every situation and circumstance is, "God what do you want in this situation now that I am here as your instrument to be used by You to show love to these people?"*

*Lord Jesus, in every situation that You came across, You saw a way in which the Father was active and because You saw the activity of the Father. You were active and You did what He would do in those situations and in those circumstances. Help me to see the Father. Help me to see what You would do. Help me to have a faith and boldness, courage and a fire as a CEO of compassion that would move me to do and to act as You would.*

*It is so easy to get caught up with activity. It is so easy to get caught up with the demands of life. But Lord, more important than all of those things is Your love being released into the earth. I believe for God-incidences; I believe for God-encounters. I believe for divine encounters with other people—God- encounters that You create, that You direct and that I am sensitive to see and hear. There is a harvest of changed lives, that not only hear the gospel but they come to Christ and they come to church and their lives are changed and their marriages are healed and their children are changed.. All because they have encountered You, the true and living God.*

*Daddy, I come in the name of Jesus and I ask that You would help Your people to dream again. Daddy, it says in the book of Joel that in the last days, when the Spirit of God was poured out, Your old men would dream dreams and Your young men would have visions. You said that Your sons and Your daughters will prophesy. These are those days; these are the days of the outpouring of your Holy Spirit that began at Pentecost and they will culminate in your return.*

*In every season, there is the opportunity for greater outpouring, with none greater than in the season leading up to the return of Christ. That means we're living in a day where the outpouring of the Holy Spirit is unprecedented and cannot be equaled and will only get greater. So God, let us have a dream and a vision for the power of the Holy Spirit being activated in us and through us revealing the truth of Your love for this earth. Make us lovers, lovers like You, filled with compassion, self-sacrificing, willing to lay down our lives for others that they might come to know You for who You are. Let our lives lift up the name of Jesus higher and higher and higher. We agree with the prophets of old. We agree with the Scriptures that said that to You, Jesus, would be the gathering of the people.*

## Day 21

## I am Justified

**"And those He predestined, He also called; and those He called, He also justified; and those He justified, He also glorified."** Romans 8:30

We have been justified through Christ. This is one of the many theological truths that shake me to my core. Let me encourage you that this truth must not be taken lightly but fully grasped. Jesus' death on the cross and the Father's receiving of His blood sacrifice means that, when God looks at me, He sees me as if I had never sinned. King David declared, "Happy is the man's whose sins freely are forgiven, his innocence has been declared by the Lord of Heaven" (Psalm 32:1). David had no idea that a day would come in which our sin would be "covered over" and we would be made new–not because of a lamb's sacrifice, but because of the shedding of Jesus' blood. Our sin nature would be crucified with Christ and we would be given a divine, righteous nature (Romans 6:2; Peter 1:3-4).

We are new creations because of the blood of Christ. We have been justified, by His blood. In layman's terms, this means, "Just as if I had never sinned." God does not see us as sinners any longer; the judgment of God does not await us or hang over our heads. We are sinless before God. We are seen as younger siblings to Jesus Himself. We are part of the family, an heir, royalty, entitled to more than we can even imagine. Our hearts should be filled with wonder, awe and praise that God would declare us His very own sons and daughters. (1 John 3:1)

What should cause such exhilaration in our hearts is that there is not one mark against us. Everything that the law declared was against us has been taken and nailed to the cross of Jesus Christ (Colossians 2:14). The blood has covered over all our sins, all our transgressions and all our wicked thoughts and desires. God has no record of them anymore.

The question must be asked then, why do we think about them so much? Why do we allow our failures and weaknesses to dominate our thinking to the point that we feel defeated and depressed? This was never God's intent; the truth of who we are now should lift us to a higher place. New Testament Christianity is marked by righteousness, peace and joy. (Romans 15:17) This is the Christians native land.

Jesus rejoiced in His knowledge that He was the Son of God. To know that God was His Father would have been the most awesome reality in the universe. But God is our Father too, and He sees us like He sees Jesus: pure and spotless, sinless and perfect. He yearns for us to come to Him with that understanding and take our rightful place in Him.

When we come before God knowing who we are, we pray with confidence and faith. There are no hurdles in our minds to get over. We come to an open heaven, just like Jesus did when He prayed. He never wondered whether or not he would get an answer to His prayers, for He knew who He was as the Father's Son. Having such oneness with the Father enabled Him to continually pray in the will of God.

*Lord, by faith I take my rightful place in You, a full blood-bought child of yours. I trust You in every situation and circumstance. You will only do what is best for me. Thank You for cleansing me of all my sins, both now and forever. I rejoice in what You have done and are doing in my life.*

Week Three

1. On Day 19 we looked at being a Warrior for our King, what did Jesus promise that He would build? Realizing that gates are defensive what will this 'built' Church do to the gates of hell?
2. Do you agree that true royalty exists to serve and not to be served? If so, how are you serving?
3. New Testament Christianity is marked by 'righteousness, peace and joy', but numerous Christians live with a mindset that steals this from them, what is that mindset?
4. What have you done to show God's love to the unsaved around you?
5. Memory Verse – quote the old ones and pick a new one

## Day 22

## The Body of Christ

**"Now you are the body of Christ, and individual members of it."**
1 Corinthians 12:27

**"The Gentiles are co-heirs, members of the same body, and partners of the promise in Christ Jesus through the gospel."** Ephesians 3:6

Jesus, in bodily form, is no longer on earth. Yet, we need Him as much now as people needed Him in the time of the gospels. Hebrews 13:8 says that Jesus Christ is the same yesterday, today and forever. God does not change; His character and will are a constant. He desires wholeness for His people and healing of our bodies, which He so accurately demonstrated in His earthly ministry. Jesus did not leave us as orphans; He has come to us by His Spirit and made us into His Body in the earth.

Just as the Ark of the Covenant was a representation of the presence and power of God, New Testament believers are a representation of the presence and power of God. Many of us have seen the movie "Raiders of the Lost Ark", a very Hollywood version of what would happen should the ark fall into the wrong hands. But little is described should the power in the ark fall into right hands. What would a person look like if the "power in the ark" resided in them? They would look like Jesus.

***"Everything of God gets expressed in him, so you can see and hear him clearly. You don't need a telescope, a microscope, or a horoscope to realize the fullness of Christ, and the emptiness of the universe without him. When you come to him, that fullness comes together for you, too. His power extends over everything"*** *Colossians2:9 (The Message)*

The ark had three things placed within it:

- The Law of God on the tablets of stone (Deuteronomy 36:26)
- A golden pot of manna (Exodus 16:32-34)

- Aaron's rod that budded, affirming his authority to be High Priest (Numbers 17)

The New Testament Believer has these signs fulfilled within him:

- The Holy Spirit writes the law of God upon our hearts to follow (Ezekiel 36:26,27)
- Jesus is the true manna that came down from heaven. we are nourished by His presence (John 6)
- The same Spirit that raised Christ from the dead raises us to newness of life anointing us for priestly duty (Romans 8:11)

God has made these signs and symbols to show us our significance to His plans and purposes in the earth. We are His presence made palpable to the people we interact with. Jesus' presence is manifested through His body, the church, through each and every believer. We are His hands, His feet, His voice, and we reveal His will. We are well able to do whatever He has asked us to do by His Spirit's enablement.

*Holy Spirit, YOU are welcome, Breath of God, Wind of Heaven overflow my life, breath on me, breath in me, breath through me. Precious Holy Spirit you are the anointing, the overflow that brings the reality of heaven into the earth. Thank You for coming to live inside of my spirit, I yearn to give YOU complete control, help me to surrender to YOUR leading and YOUR guiding, make me an instrument in YOUR for the Father's Glory.*

## Day 23

## I am Royalty

**"And hast made us unto our God kings and priests: and we shall reign on the earth."** Revelation 5:10 (King James Version)

Some years ago, when my children were in their preteens, I was crying out to God to be a better father. My father passed away when I was nine and that left a huge lack in my life, particularly in the arena of having an image to learn from and to follow. My dad was in the army; though he was a strict disciplinarian he also expressed his love. The easiest way that I can say it is that he was a great balance of the two; he always set a standard, but lovingly enforced it. But there were so many dynamics that were lost in not having him here to assist me.

God did something amazing inside of me through the loss and the pain, however. He showed me in my first year of salvation that He had covenanted with orphans to Father them. I cried out to God with all my heart, "Father Me!" and He has in the good times and the bad, in favor and in discipline. I have seen what could have been the most devastating event in my life turned into a grace and strength to be a father of honor to His praise and glory.

While praying for the ability to father my children, knowing that Jesus followed His Father's example in all that He did and said, I was asking for more of God's heart in how to interact with my children. God began to speak to my heart about how He treats me like royalty and that, because I am a co-heir with Jesus, He is working in me to rule and reign with Him. This is real to God for He sees eternity and what we will do with Him for eternity. God knows the future and He knows what I will need in the future to accomplish His perfect plan and purpose for my life. Being a master planner, God has already worked into our lives the gifting we will need to fulfill His purposes. Now He also works the character we will need to enable us not to forfeit the blessings that will come into our lives.

As God was speaking this to my heart, I could see He was laying out a plan for me and my interaction with my children. In a nutshell, "Treat them like royalty. You have a princess and two princes that you are raising." You are preparing them to rule and reign in life. How are you getting them ready for their role of blessing and ministry in life? Lessons this straight forward, once instilled in their hearts, will enable them to make right decisions for their future.

- Your Attitude will determine whether you will achieve greatness or live beneath your destiny.
- God chose you to lead, created you to be a dignitary; accept the call and prepare for greatness.
- Royalty is entitled to certain privileges, but much greater responsibility.
- Royalty is honored and held in great esteem when its heart is to minister to its people and not to be ministered to. Royalty exists to serve not to be served.

It is not by chance that, from Abraham all the way to the last kings that ruled in Judah and Israel, we are confronted with kings and queens throughout scripture. Proverbs prepares princes to be kings; Samuel through Chronicles details living examples of what to do and what not to do; and the prophets ministered before kings to give them and the nation the word of God. Quite simply, if your father is king, you are entitled to a throne. Our Father is King of the universe. Satan is a usurper who had for a season usurped our rightful place to rule and reign in the earth and in particular over him. King Jesus has set it right and now we can with power and authority declare His purposes in the earth.

*King Jesus, teach me how to walk out my high calling. Teach me to have Your heartbeat toward the responsibility You are placing and will place on my shoulders. More than anything let my life shine Your name and Your glory.*

## Day 24

### Carriers of His Presence

**"For God who said, "Let light shine out of darkness," has shone in our hearts to give the light of the knowledge of God's glory in the face of Jesus Christ. Now we have this treasure in clay jars, so that this extraordinary power may be from God and not from us. "** 2 Corinthians 4:6-7

What is our identity? What makes us different from anybody else on the planet? All of the truths that we have been looking at speak to who we are and how we can glory and exalt in God for making us and saving us. We are unique, special, highly favored and blessed by God. We should be overjoyed at being who we are and we should never desire to be anyone else. We are saints; we are righteous; we are salt; we are light; we are heirs; we are royalty; we are anointed. Today we will look at something that has meaning and relevance when we learn to walk in this truth.

God established the Tabernacle of Moses on Mt. Sinai so that He could dwell with His people. The most important piece of the Tabernacle was called the Ark of the Covenant or the Ark of His Presence. No artifact in the entire world could equal its significance. The significance of the Ark was that it symbolized the throne of God on the earth and the presence of God with His people. When Israel as a nation saw the cloud of fire by night and the cloud of glory by day, they knew the presence of God was with them and that they were protected. When Israel moved into the Promised Land and the glory cloud hovered over the Ark of the Covenant, Israel was at peace knowing that God's glory and presence was with them to enable them to succeed and to overcome. Never did they dream that a day would come when God Himself would allow Jerusalem to be overthrown and the ark disappears from them and from history.

Now, Jesus was the living embodiment of the Ark of the Covenant, for the Holy Spirit dwelt on Him without measure (John 3:34). He was the fullness of the Godhead bodily (Colossians 2:9) and so typified the wood of the ark in His humanity and the gold of the ark His divinity. He is the literal fulfillment of the ark.

As we consider what He has done, we recognize that in dying on the cross, rending the veil, and establishing a new covenant, we are now endowed with the Holy Spirit. No longer is it only priests, kings, prophets and judges who are anointed, but now every New Testament believer is filled with the glory cloud of His presence in the person of the Holy Spirit. We have this treasure, the glory of God, in the face of Jesus Christ, in clay jars or as the old King James used to say in earthen vessels Clay jars were in Biblical economy the primary way in which liquids were stored and moved in. They were common, ordinary, everywhere and the external was not an indicator of what was within. On jar might contain oil or water or frankincense, each with a different value. Now God looks at us and we are like clay jars, truly earthen vessels, but He places Himself within. (2 Corinthians 4:7). There is glory on you and glory in you because of the awesome wonder and awe of the Holy Spirit within.

*Mighty God, YOU are with me, YOU live inside of me, YOUR presence abides. How I long to unlock YOUR presence and YOUR power to the world around me. I rejoice in the truth of YOUR abiding presence. Give me ears to hear what YOU are speaking to the Church and I thank YOU for a heart to obey.*

## Day 25

### Sheep of His Pasture

**"Acknowledge that Yahweh is God. He made us, and we are His —His people, the sheep of His pasture".** Psalm 100:3

Sheep need help. They are notorious for getting themselves into trouble. They have no natural defences and are therefore helpless against predators. They are famous for so over eating a given area that left to themselves; they would eventually starve to death. They need help to live and to succeed in the most ordinary aspects of life. No intelligent person would want to be likened to sheep, and yet God unashamedly declares loud and clear that we are all like sheep that have gone astray. Sheep are famous for wandering. Even though everything they have need of is before them, they still take to wandering unless they are shepherded from themselves.

It is not by coincidence in Luke 17 that the story of the Lost Sheep and the Prodigal Son are mentioned together. Jesus said many times that He was the Good Shepherd who came to seek and to save the lost. If 99 sheep were safe at home and one was lost, off He would go to bring back the one into the fold. How much love and care does God give to us in recognition of our perpetual propensity to wander off? How frustrating would that be if you had a loved one who simply refused to stay put but kept looking for greener grass in another field? God promises to heal us of our backsliding so that we can live in right relationship with Him.

We have the blessed opportunity to be sheep in Christ's pasture. There is no pasture like His pasture. No other Shepherd has the nail scars that our Shepherd has. The test of a true shepherd was their willingness to lay down their lives for the sheep. Whether a shepherd stayed and fought or whether a shepherd ran away told everything that needed to be known about that individual. Jesus took on the lion, the bear and the giant and defeated them all, but with great cost. Our Shepherd has proven again and again the greatness of His love. I am so grateful to be purchased by Him and to look to Him for direction, comfort, refreshing, washing, protection, food and relationship.

Stay in His pasture, never leave. With all the 'fields' out there and all the voices that will be calling your name to try and get you to accept their mantras and their philosophies, simply remember that not one of them has nail-scarred hands, nail-scarred feet and a spear-pierced side. King Jesus proved ultimately that He loves us more than any other could.

*Daddy, I choose to stay in Your pasture, under Your loving care. You offer a table unequaled in its ability to feed and nourish my spirit, my soul and my body. David the great Psalmist declares that you will actually prepare a table for me in the presence of my enemies. In the most difficult and dangerous times of my life YOU are there and YOU are providing nourishment, strength and refreshing. I choose to stay at YOUR table and be blessed.*

## Day 26

### Branches of the Vine

**"I am the vine; you are the branches. The one who remains in Me and I in him produces much fruit, because you can do nothing without Me.** John 15:5

In Canada right now, the winter months are just about to begin. Days have been shorter and nights have been longer and temperatures are declining. The trees are dropping their leaves preparing for their winter nap.

Sometimes over the winter season, wind and snow storms come and branches get broken or severed from the tree. When that happens, the branch withers and dies and bears no fruit. This illustration is readily understood around the world. In the Bible, Jesus tells us He is the vine and we are the branches. If we stay connected, we will bear much fruit. Without that connection, we will bear nothing.

No matter how intelligent or rich or praised and lauded we are, we are dependent on God for life and for fruitfulness. Everything we have depends on the blessing and the favour of God, whether we recognize it or not. God is gracious and merciful and good and causes these blessings to fall on the just and the unjust as He deems fit. Our dependence unlocks the door to our potential. We cannot try to produce spiritual fruitfulness on our own or through our own strength or human intellect, for lasting fruit is a work of the Spirit. When we are dependent, trusting, submitted and willing to give God all the praise and glory then we can be mightily used by Him to bring forth much fruit.

We remain in Jesus by our heart attitude of dependence on Him and by our commitment to prayerful communion and worship, particularly when we fail to understand what He is doing (Job 1:20-22). We also remain in Jesus by our commitment to His Word's answer to our dilemmas and by our obedience to His Spirit and Word. This is where Christianity gets really exciting because it is not a dead form of religion we are following or merely a set of rules and regulations on life; it is a living, vital, earth-changing relationship.

One day, a man named Ananias was praying in his room when God spoke to him. God told him to go to a house on a certain day and pray for a certain man. God told him that when he prayed, this man would be loosed from blindness, filled with the Holy Spirit and would become one of the greatest Christian leaders of all times. Ananias resisted at first, knowing that the man was a murdering persecutor of Christians. But God said, "No, he is a chosen vessel." Ananias obeyed and Saul became Paul through the wondrous working of God in the earth. True Christian living is marked by continual divine encounters of God's workings through us. This comes from being connected to the vine.

*Gracious God, I am so happy to be connected to You, to have the ability to remain in You and know that You remain in me. This is the promise of Your great Word and You cannot lie. I want to live a life of fruitfulness and I know that I can and I will as I remain in You. I unlock the doors for You to come on out and minister life, healing and salvation to those all around.*

## Day 27

## Chosen by Love

**"You did not choose me, but I chose you. I appointed you that you should go out and produce fruit and that your fruit should remain, so that whatever you ask the Father in My name, He will give you."** John 15:16

When a letter comes in the mail from the government or from royalty, it perks our attention. I know for a fact the one time I saw a Christmas card invitation from the Nigerian High Embassy, I was extremely impressed. I was so impressed that I got out my camera and took a picture of it to commemorate the occasion, even though the card wasn't for me. Just to see the card and to hold it and to take it all in was quite momentous. To this point, only once in my 49 years of life have I held such a card in my hand. The recipient was not nearly as thrilled as I was. She grew up an ambassador's daughter and the pomp and circumstance of her life was ordinary for her, but not for me. My point is that the thrill of that High Embassy invitation to a Christmas *party* in Uganda was only for a select few in the entire country. You would only be invited by special invitation and to try and be chosen would simply be impossible. Those chosen knew that they were special, that they were dignitaries, royalty or somehow connected to them.

Many of us will never be invited to such an event. We may never even be considered for such an event. If we were honest, we have felt different forms of rejection because we have been overlooked for special events, birthday parties, being a part of the "in" group, jobs or involvement in other things for which we are more than qualified. BUT God has chosen us and ordained us to a high and holy calling. God has chosen us to be His very own vice-regents on the planet, expressing His Kingdom and glory to the world around us. Each and every one of us should feel that we have been appointed by God to do is of great significance and importance.

There is no higher calling than to be chosen by God to work in His service. I am not talking about being ordained to full-time ministry as a profession, for in reality every Christian has this high and holy call to reach the world around us. I am thrilled to be called of God and chosen by Him. His royal invitation comes sealed with the Holy Spirit and paid for with the blood of the prince and heir of the Kingdom, King Jesus. I am honored and highly favored to have been chosen by God to go and bear fruit for His Kingdom, in character, in gifting and with souls. I am overwhelmed at the goodness of God that He would include me in His ambassadorship, but I take it with great joy and expectation of His glory accompanying me.

God has a purpose for our lives and He handmade us and designed us with gifts to be used in our calling to bear fruit for His glory. We may take great courage in knowing that when we need anything, we can get it from our eternal bank account. That account has been made available to us as we are about our Father's business.

*Daddy, thank You for the calling and for the ordination to manifest Your love to the world around us. I know as I follow the leading of your Holy Spirit the fruit will remain. My significance lies in the truth of how much YOU love me and my significance to YOUR plans and purposes for my life. I have been chosen by YOU, I have been appointed by YOU therefore my life has significance and purpose from beginning to end.*

## Day 28

## Victorious

**"Now thanks be to God who always leads us in triumph in Christ, and through us diffuses the fragrance of His knowledge in every place."** 2 Corinthians 2:14

Thanksgiving is one of the weapons of our warfare that protects our attitude from the attacks of the enemy of our soul. When our hearts are filled with thanksgiving, what will follow is that we will have great protection against depression, worry, fear and anxiety. Thanksgiving declares that we know that God will supply our needs according to His riches in glory, not based on our works but on His love and our trust in Him (Philippians 4:19).

The Word of God says that God always, always, always leads us in TRIUMPH in Christ. Right at the outset there are two truths that we can learn from this.

One, God must be in the driver's seat. That speaks of Lordship. "He da Boss", not you or me at any time. He is sovereign, He is all-knowing, He is all-powerful, and He sees the end from the beginning. We submit to His Lordship, knowing He will never give us more than we can handle. We take the position of victory from the beginning to the end. "Lean not on your own understanding but in all your ways acknowledge Him and He will direct your paths" (Proverbs 3:4-6).

The Word of God also says that the triumph is in Christ, which is an emphasis on the anointing or person of the Holy Spirit. We must be in Christ, living in the anointing, being led and guided by the Holy Spirit. We cannot win spiritual battles with carnal weapons. We cannot achieve spiritual victories in our own strength or by our merits. We simply disqualify for the victory when we try to accomplish God's will with man's strength or wisdom.

The greatest lesson in scripture concerning this is when David tried to bring up the Ark of the Covenant, man's way or the way of the Gentiles. God had ordained in the law that the priests were to carry the ark of God on their shoulders. God had allowed the Philistines to transport the ark on a cart, because they were ignorant of the Law. When David did it as though he were ignorant of the Law, what happened was death resulted. This caused David to wonder how He would be able to have the presence of the Lord in Jerusalem. (2 Sam. 6) But as soon as David did God's will God's way he received God's blessing.

David's desire was that the presence of God would fill Jerusalem and all Israel. God's will has always been that His presence fill the earth and now because of the indwelling Holy Spirit God's desire is being fully realized. For He makes His glorious presence known through us wherever we are. He diffuses the awesome awareness of who He is through us as we live in the victory that He has won for us. People know there is something different about us immediately. They see that we look different, talk differently, react differently and believe differently. When Christ is on the inside, He reveals Himself on the outside. Our countenance is affected by our glorious interaction with Him. In the same way that the face of Moses shone with His glory in the Old Testament and the face of Stephen shone with His glory in the New Testament, so our faces can shine as we are those who live out of the secret place.

*Daddy, I give you the reins of my life. You are in charge. You take the lead; I will follow. I submit my will to your will and know that no weapon formed against me is greater than the one who lives in me. I am with You and You are with me so my victory is assured.*

## Day 29

## Vessels of Honor

**"Now in a large house there are not only gold and silver bowls, but also those of wood and clay, some for honorable use, some for dishonorable. So if anyone purifies himself from anything dishonorable, he will be a special instrument, set apart, useful to the Master, prepared for every good work".** 2 Timothy 2:20-21

What kind of vessel do you want to be? God is looking for a certain kind of life that He can use. Every one of us will one day stand before God and give an account for the lives that we have lived. This is what the Bible calls "the judgment seat of Christ". (2 Corinthians 5:10). This causes us to look at our lives from eternity backwards.

What do I mean by this? I mean that instead of looking forward so that I can get the most out of my life, I live my life always mindful of standing before the judgement seat of Christ. When I stand there I desire to receive the rewards He has destined for me. I cannot wait till my life is almost over to plan for that day. I must live everyday with that revelation in mind. If I live like that, then I am assured that I will be a golden vessel of honor that God has been able to use.

Let's take a minute and look at this from a different perspective as well. In your view you might see yourself represented as a wooden spoon. The mundane ordinary faithfulness of life seems to be wooden at its very best. We think that if we are on the pulpit or if we are famous or if everybody knows our name, that must be a gold vessel and will receive greater reward. But God looks at the heart, the motives and our obedience. He looks to see whether or not we fulfill our potential.

Down here, someone might look like gold and someone might look like wood. But wait until it passes through God's fire. When our works pass through heaven's fire test, God will determine what our works are made of.

We determine the outcome now. We cannot wait to a later date and say, "Now I will begin to live right and do everything that will I know I should to earn a glorious reward on that day." No, right now is the time to live to the fullest. We have been called to the Kingdom for such a time as this to make an eternal difference to those we are connected to.

Let me share a quick story with you. A newly saved janitor was cleaning. He had recently been filled with the Spirit and so, with great excitement as he cleaned the basement, he was speaking in tongues to the Lord. He did not know that he was being overheard by someone who could interpret what he was saying because the tongue that he was using, unbeknownst to him, was Spanish. The man did not know what the Holy Spirit was praying through him but the Holy Spirit was praying to the Father to fill him up with more of the Holy Spirit, to let his life overflow with power, let him be one that would be used to lay hands on the sick and see them recover, open the eyes of the blind, open the ears of the deaf. "Let him be a mighty catalyst that stirs others to see the reality of who We are, that they too might be involved in the glory of preaching the gospel to those that do not at this time know Us." The man who overheard was mightily convicted and from that day on viewed prayer from a very different perspective. He immediately began believing God for miracles and signs and wonders and power because, all of a sudden, he understood that God desires this for his people.

The issue I believe is usefulness. We are to bear fruit. God cannot pray to God that we would be fruitless or that His power would not be used in our lives. Jesus paid the price so that the Church would be activated in glory and power. Such lives would truly be lives of honor and not lives of dishonor.

*Daddy, I pray that You would continue to lift my vision so that it would be Yours, that I would see things from Your perspective and I would dream Your dream. I recognize that I one day will stand before You and give account for my life. I tell you now that I want to be, on that day, a vessel of honor that has lived in such a way that you so gloriously anticipate my Arrival.*

## Day 30

## Anointed

**"But you have an anointing from the Holy One, and you all have knowledge."** 1 John 2:20

**Now the One who confirms us with you in Christ, and has anointed us, is God** 2 Corinthians 1:21

Today, we want to look at the Divine Person of the Holy Spirit. In the scriptures, the Holy Spirit is clearly revealed to us. When Jesus was baptized in the Jordon River by John, the Holy Spirit, as a dove, descended on Him. From this point on, Jesus was no longer known only as the son of Mary and Joseph, but as Jesus the Christ, or Yeshua Hamashea – Jesus, the Anointed One. Scripture makes it clear that the fullness of the anointing on Jesus was unprecedented and was without measure and never left (John 1: 32; 3:34).

The anointing is synonymous with the person of the Holy Spirit. The scriptures we are looking at today identify us as being anointed as well. The Holy Spirit indwells the believer and enables the believer to know and to do the will of God. But even more significantly the person of the Holy Spirit with His gifts and fruit enables us to partner supernaturally with God and expect to see miracles, signs and wonders in our lives for His glory and His glory alone.

The Kingdom of which you are a part is a supernatural Kingdom that reveals the God of the whole universe. God creates and sustains life itself. Without faith, we know that it is impossible to please God, but that faith is not just salvation faith it is also a faith that opens the door into the supernatural working of God in the earth. In the days and weeks that lie ahead, you will find God answering your prayers in miraculous ways. Don't be surprised; instead, every time you pray, expect God to answer your prayers more and more as you pray for His Kingdom to come and for His will to be done in the earth. As we have seen already, we are ambassadors of heaven on earth to represent the King of Kings.

The currency of heaven is not material but spiritual; the authority of heaven manifests itself in the earth through miraculous means vindicating the power of God to affect the material world through the spiritual. We have the authority of God resident in us to release His will in the earth so that those who do not know who He is and what He is like can come to grips with His reality.

God’s will has always been that we represent Him to the world around us. People are groaning to see what life was really supposed to be like and we are privileged to show them (Romans 8:22-23). The anointing of the Holy Spirit that was on Jesus destroyed the works of the enemy and brought people out of darkness into light through numerous good works, signs, wonders and miracles. God has not changed His desire to bless and to heal. It is our calling to take up the same anointing and to minister God's love. Yes, it is too much for us but it is not too much for Him.

*Daddy, all of scripture is filled with Your miraculous dealings with mankind. Every book of the Bible records Your activity, whether it is protecting Your people, supplying provision, healing the sick or changing hearts. It seems that You were always doing something that revealed Your will and who You were. Seeing that You never change, I believe for the same experiences in and through my life.*

## Day 31

### Racially Chosen

**"But you are a chosen race, a royal priesthood, a holy nation, a people for God's own possession, that you may proclaim the excellencies of Him who has called you out of darkness into His marvelous light."** 1 Peter 2:8

I want to take a little time and look at the statement in the Word of God that says that we are a brand new race of people. We are a race of people that did not exist before. There was a time when there was no genus of people and then, after the stunning event of Calvary, a new group of people began to inhabit planet earth. This race of people consists of all races of people, for it is not a biological group of people but a spiritual body of people.

God made the nations because He glories in diversity. Look at the flowers, the trees, the birds and the bees. Look at how every snowflake is different. When God made mankind, He preordained the racial ethnicity of humanity. When He did, He said "It is very good." , only after the creation of mankind did God say it was 'very good' (Genesis 1:31)

Now, if only our interactions with each other were based on these truths, the racial wars that have gone on for millennia would never have ever taken place. So many times, man's inhumanity to others is based on race. The deeper issue, however, is not skin but sin. Our own insecurities, fears and prejudices cause us to treat someone different from us in a very hurtful and sinful way.

God, who liked what He did in the first place, added another race made up of every race: the Christian race. The Christian race of people is to mirror Jesus' culture and not man's culture. We are to embody heaven's Identity and not just the identity of the world. When we look and act like the world, we lose our ability to influence them in a God way. But when we mirror God's Kingdom way of living, the world cannot help but stop and take notice.

God's way is inclusive of all tribes, nations and tongues. God tells us that He is no respecter of persons. The person who loves and obeys God will be honored by Him. When we extend that to each other, the truth of God's love is manifested for all to see.

Though the history of Christianity has the black mark of racism in it, this is a new day of revelation and understanding as God pours out His Spirit. He enables us to show who Christ truly is as we love one another as Christ loved us. When we see the races of people functioning in unity, we stop and look and listen. We are intrigued and want to know what exactly is taking place.

God's plan of salvation was first to the Jews and then to the Gentiles. The disciples had God's message in mind for the Jewish people only. But as the Spirit of God began to move and save, heal, deliver and baptize Gentiles in the Holy Spirit, the disciples' eyes were opened to the scriptures that were there all the time proclaiming salvation to the Gentiles. One body, one faith, one Lord, one Church—when we live like this, the races will come in and join the Christian race.

*God, what a great day to be alive, as all walls of racism are being obliterated in the church because of what You did on the cross. Thank You that You have made us all one and we through our oneness can show the world who You truly are.*

## Week Four

1. If Christianity is not a religion than what exactly is it?
2. Does God still do miracles today? Who does He use to accomplish them?
3. You have been chosen by God to go and do what?
4. Is there any people group that you have "issues" with? What do you believe God would have you do about that?
5. Take a moment and flip through each devotional of this month and for each lesson ask yourself the above question, does this Identity in Christ speak to my Acceptance, my Security or my Significance.
6. Memory Verse – John 15:16

## Day 32

## Communion

**"Then the LORD said, "Should I hide what I am about to do from Abraham?"** (Genesis 18:17)

For the next 33 days, we are going to look at the topic of prayer. The word I prefer to use is *communion*. Not like the communion table, if you are familiar with that, but more to the root meaning of the word. One definition of communion would be the "interchange or sharing of thoughts or emotions; intimate communication." 5

The very heart and core of prayer is intimate communication. As you become a student of the Word of God, you will find that this is the cornerstone of your relationship with God—intimate honest heart felt communication. It is the kind of prayer that does not conform to religiosity, but is first and foremost personal. The beautiful reality of this is that it is two-way communication. We speak to God and we also hear God speaking to us.

Synonyms of the word "commune" are these: participation, togetherness, association, fellowship, persuasion, and closeness. 6 All of these are an absolute must if prayer is to be anything like what the Bible teaches that it should be.

Please remember God is not interested in religion. God desires to be in a love affair with us. If there is anything that great lovers do it is communicate their hearts to each other. They know each other intimately and they delight in bringing joy to the one they love. Communicating their love is their delight.

God also delights in communicating His love. He does it in the sunshine, in the rain, in the moon's glow and in the stars twinkle. He does it all throughout creation, but He also does it in personal ways through the "God-incidences" that come into our lives. The deer we see in the middle of a city, the unexpected financial gift, the memory that lifts our day, the sale of a car, the healing of a loved one–this list could go on infinitum. These are all God's ways of saying, "I see you and I love you and if I did not spare my own Son, but freely gave Him up for you, how shall I not with Him also freely give you all things" (Romans 8:32). That's our Daddy!

Abraham, a man of God, was going about his daily activities one day when God Himself decided to pay him an extraordinary visit. It was an amazing visit because, during this time, God confirmed a 24-year old promise that would be fulfilled a year later. In Genesis 18:17, God says, "Should I hide what I am about to do from Abraham?" God goes on to say that He will reveal to Abraham why He came down because Abraham was an obedient, godly man who ordered all aspects of his life in a way that was pleasing to God.

Abraham is called the "friend of God" and that is something we should aspire to be as well. God through Jesus not only calls us friends, He makes us family. Remember, we have been adopted. God is our Daddy, so can we substitute our name with Abraham's in the above question?

There is no doubt in my mind that God desires to commune with us in the same way as He did with Abraham. God and Abraham partnered together in the outcome of what was about to happen on earth. God is still partnering with those who seek Him and put Him first, who cry out believing for God to come and influence the world through them. Are you prepared to hear what He has to say that will affect the world around you?

*Daddy, I want to know Your heart more, I desire to be a son/daughter who will bring You glory and praise. I know in Jesus I make Your heart glad, teach me how to pray for Your Glory to be revealed. I, like, Abraham want to be an influencer in the outcome of Your will on the earth. I want to draw near to You and live a life of communion. Help me always to have a heart to hear and obey what You are speaking.*

5 communion. Dictionary.com. *Dictionary.com Unabridged.* Random House, Inc.http://dictionary.reference.com/browse/communion (accessed: July 01, 2013).

6. ibid

## Day 33

## Inclusivity

**"Our Father in heaven,"** Matthew 6:9c

When Jesus begins to teach His disciples how to pray, the first word that He uses is the word "Our". Say it a couple of times, in your mind and then out loud. We are talking absolute total inclusion here, not exclusion. We are looking at this prayer by phrase, in order to do this we have to stop before we go ahead and ask this question. Can He actually truly mean "our" – in an inclusive sense?

There are some 6800 to 6900 different distinct languages in the world today according to the Ethnologue.7 Now if we translate the Word of God into every language and any one of these individuals were to read Matthew 6 and hear Jesus teaching us how to pray and He tells us – OUR – any given person is given opportunity to pray, to petition God, to acknowledge God opens His arms to have them come to Him. Muslim, Hindu, Atheist, Agnostic, Buddhist, Animist or Hedonist—we are all included in Jesus' magnificent "our". We are all part of the human race and, therefore, all part of the human family. God, who created us, now includes us and says to all mankind everywhere, "I am waiting for you to come and pray to Me."

John 21:17 "Don't cling to Me," Jesus told her, "for I have not yet ascended to the Father. But go to My brothers and tell them that I am ascending to My Father and your Father—to My God and your God."

If you stop and think about it for a moment, all of humanity is one family, the human family that started with God when He made Adam and Eve and placed them in Eden. All of us are related because we have the same natural and spiritual source. Sin is what separated us from our love affair with Father God. We are children of God by creation, but God designed us for so much more. He has revealed the way for all of us to come to Him as Father by sending His Son to die in our place and provide a way for us to be Adopted sons and daughters of God. Through Jesus we are children of God not just by creation but by actual adoption. And so, as Jesus is teaching on prayer, He starts by saying "Our Father". When He is preparing to ascend after the cross, He again affirms the depth of the love God has for us and the relationship He is calling us into. Jesus says He is preparing to return to my Father and your Father; He, in many ways, makes us equal with Himself, co-heirs, joint-heirs, those who will share in His glory and splendor.

Jesus elevates us to family status as brothers and sisters, sons and daughters—an intimate personal loving relationship between God and us. When we come to God in prayer, we are coming to our source, our progenitor, our Abba, our Papa—who just happens to be the God of the universe and of all creation, natural and spiritual. He is the universe architect and we get to call Him Daddy.

God invites you in. He identifies with you, with your condition, and knows you by name.

*Father, I thank You that You make Yourself available to all who would call out to You. It is amazing to consider that You are our source of life and, although we may vary in color, in language, in culture and in so many other ways, prayer unifies all humanity. Prayer is the only way to get to God. Knowing that all men must come to You the same way unifies the human condition. You are no respecter of faces. You love us all the same. It is faith that moves You. Thanks for loving us with perfect love.*

*Pray as you feel in your heart to.*

7 Lewis, M. Paul, Gary F. Simons, and Charles D. Fennig (eds.). 2013. *Ethnologue: Languages of the World, Seventeenth edition.* Dallas, Texas: SIL International. Online version: http://www.ethnologue.com.

## Day 34

## Daddy God

**"And because you are sons, God has sent the Spirit of His Son into our hearts, crying, "*Abba*, Father!" 7 So you are no longer a slave but a son, and if a son, then an heir through God."** Galatians 4:6, 7

The family of mankind has a Father that loves us and dearly longs for us to come to Him as His very own child. I lost my father when I was nine. I yearned from that day to be a father and to have children. I am a blessed father of three children, a daughter and two sons.

Children approach parents differently than they approach anybody else. In a healthy home, parents and children share their hearts openly. They have times of very intimate conversation and prayer. Wisdom and guidance are communicated for the present and the future. Not just anybody can receive that ongoing love and care. Religion produces slaves but a true Christian experience, including true biblical discipleship, will produce sons and heirs.

Most religious experiences produce a form of religious slavery that ensnares the participants to a system of religion that never frees the soul to truly experience God. There is always another hoop to jump through, always another job to do, always another prayer to pray or a fast to fulfill, always more money to give to be a better more mature "believer, disciple, Christian" - because God is worthy. Make no mistake, it all sounds wonderful and good and is backed up with myriads of scriptures, but the "believer"' never arrives. The yoke is not easy and the burden is not light. God as Abba, Daddy, intimately drawing you into a love relationship, seems just as distant as it did before you were saved. And yet Paul warns that what the Jews experienced before Christ was slavery. Now that they are in Christ, they are to experience sonship and royalty.

Why do we do what we do? Why do we tithe? Why do we fast? Why do we commit ourselves to a life of devotions of prayer and the word? Why do we share our faith? Do we do it to gain acceptance, to be a better Christian, to obey the Bible, to get a reward in heaven and maybe earn some more blessings and favor down here on earth? Do we do it to prove that we are truly saved, because those more mature than us told us it is the right thing to do? Are any of these answers truly wrong?

We are sons/daughters of God. We are like our Father. Our Father is Love and Love gives and gives and gives and gives with no thought of getting anything in return. Love gives time and love gives money and love drives one to know the beloved more. Love can't help but talk about the beloved. Love naturally denies itself for others. The gospel of Jesus Christ is all about love. When the love is missing, the form and ritual remain but the power is gone. So Jesus stands outside of His own Church and knocks to come in (Revelation 2:20). Churches function for years and don't even know that the presence of God is missing. Sadly, they don't know He is gone for they never ever really had Him. Religion not only misses Him when He shows up, it ends up persecuting and crucifying the true moves of God for true love is just too radical for them.

In Ephesians 3:17, Paul prays that we would know the love of Jesus which surpasses knowledge. It is not knowledge of the love of God that God desires for us, but the experience of it that transforms us and moulds us into His image. The more you experience and personally know God's love the more you desire that others know Him as well. Love, above all else gives, desiring nothing in return. Love by nature, gives and gives and gives, always seeking the best for the loved one.

In the ensuing months, you can be sure that the very person of the Godhead will be wooing you to Himself so that you will be rooted and grounded in His love. Everything about this journal is to help you develop a lifelong devotional life in which communing/loving/worshipping God is the very apex of your life.

*Thank You Lord, for the communion that I have already been enjoying with You. My heart's cry is to go deeper into Your love and into giving that love away. Help me to be an open channel for the current of Your love to flow through me. Fill my heart to overflowing so that who You are will always be seen in me. I am so blessed to call you Abba and to know Your great love for me. In Jesus name, amen.*

## Day 35

## The Greatest Name of All

**"Our Father in heaven, your name be honored as holy"** Matthew 6:9

ames speak of character, authority, honor and worth. A name identifies the essence of the item or person being described. God's name, therefore, must be treated differently than any other name. Within the Ten Commandments, we see that God's name must be honored, respected and not taken in vain—the opposite of the way everybody in our day and age uses His name.

God's names and titles supersede all others. The very term "holy" means to be set apart or separate, telling us first and foremost that there is one God and, in all the universe, there is none that can compare to Him. Dr. Lockwood declared "the heaven of heavens cannot contain Him, let alone a man explains Him." He is so worthy of praise and honor and glory! Scripture is filled with scenes of heaven and, every time we are given a glimpse into eternity, we see the cherubim, the seraphim, the archangels and angels all worshipping the God of glory.

We are made to worship and the Father is seeking worshippers (John 4:23-24). You cannot come into God's presence without a worshipful heart. We enter the gates of heaven with thanksgiving and we into the courtroom of glory with praise (Psalm 100:4). When we come into that awe-filled place, we can do nothing but adore. Prayer can only be monumental when it is centered on God and it is only centered on God when we come in worship to Him. Sing to Him because He is worthy. Invest time in worship as you begin your prayer time. The power of this devotion is that your praise and worship will lift your mind from the earthly to the heavenly, from the temporal to the eternal, from the natural to the spiritual, and prayers will flow like a torrent of love.

When I gave my heart to the Lord, I would pray for extended times every evening before bed. The old hymn "Heaven Came Down and Glory Filled my Soul" would aptly describe what would happen every single evening. I was a boy who could not hold a note and who had a terrible voice, but I would sing for hours—hymns, children's songs and new choruses—because my heart was so filled with love for the God who saved me.

God would respond. His presence would fill my times with Him. He would speak to my heart and He would direct my prayers. Though I did not know I was fulfilling scriptural principles of how to approach God's presence, the results were life-altering. Now that I know the principles, I desire that every child of God enjoy the communion and presence that Jesus' death on the cross has made available to us. He alone is worthy of worship. Let us never fail to give Him all the glory and praise He is due.

We honor the name of God by giving Him the praise and worship that He deserves. You cannot truly spend time in worship every day and then go out and live a wanton life. As Christians, our desire is to honor God's name in every aspect of our lives. We hurt inside when others dishonor the name of God but we know that we are part of the solution. Live worthy of His name.

*"Oh how I love Jesus; oh how I love Jesus; oh how I love Jesus; Because He first loved me.*"

## Day 36

## Kingdom Restored

**"Your Kingdom Come, Your will be done on earth as it is in heaven."** Matthew 6:10

What did the disciples and listeners think when they heard these words? What were they already praying for that would correspond to this line of thinking? The Jews of Jesus' day were waiting for the Messiah to come to usher in God's Kingdom on earth through a literal king who would sit upon the throne of Israel, conquer all of Israel's enemies and restore the nation to the glory and splendor of David and Solomon. They were looking for a literal, natural king and kingdom. Every Jewish person prayed and believed in this and many still do.

Jesus was referring to a different Kingdom, however; it was spiritual in its orientation before it was natural. God's kingdom does change the natural kingdoms of this world, but not by war as was the case in the Old Testament. This King starts by ruling and reigning in hearts and lives. When we speak of Kingdoms we speak of kings, of royalty, of authority, of reigning and of ruling. Jesus is asking us to pray for His Kingdom, where He sits as King of Kings and Lord of Lords, to cover over planet earth. For the heartbeat of Jesus to be fulfilled in in every aspect of life, we can ask, "What would King Jesus do?" In doing it, we bring more of His Kingdom into the earth.

When Jesus left the planet, He told us that all authority and power had been given to Him. (Matthew 28:19) In the ministry of the disciples before the cross they brought healing and deliverance to people, but they left the preaching and teaching to Jesus. After the cross and after the Baptism of the Holy Spirit they fully grasped the message of the Kingdom and now were able to 'make disciples of all nations. The New Testament church in its inaugural years began to transform cities and nations, bringing them to a place of freedom from sin and unrighteousness. The purpose of every church is to do the same and we begin in prayer, agreeing with heaven's heart beat to come down and bless all mankind.

The more we know God's heart, the more we can pray for His Kingdom, His rule and His reign to come into the circumstances of our lives. Jesus came to reveal who God really is and what He Himself would do if He were walking down here on the earth. He healed the sick, cleansed the lepers, opened blind eyes, raised the dead, restored families, healed marriages, forgave sinners and lifted the humble to places of prominence while dethroning the proud. Jesus' ministry is a picture of what God's kingdom is full of. If we were to break it down to its lowest common denominator, it would be "help"—help to get man back to where he was before sin came in and ruined God's plan for man to be coheirs with Christ, ruling and reigning (Genesis1:26-27).

*God, count me in. Rule first in my life, reign in my heart, let me be under Your authority and work in me and through me to see Your glorious Kingdom revealed in the earth. .My prayer is that I would be integrally involved in manifesting Your Kingdom and by doing so fulfilling Your will.*

## Day 37

## Surrender

**"Father, if You are willing, take this cup away from Me—nevertheless, not My will, but Yours, be done."** Luke 22:42

Human nature is noted for its strong will to do what it pleases and not as it is told. In movies, mankind is praised for its single-minded desire to overcome all obstacles and survive, whether the enemy is aliens, illness, apocalyptic designs or extreme weather. Man always finds a way to conquer the foe and win. Man's determination to succeed or overcome is noted throughout our history and we can see how we believe in our own invincibility.

Have you ever had a disagreement with your parents, your boss or your spouse? Have you ever been asked to do something that you simply did not want to do and felt totally inconvenienced by the request? Can you look in the mirror of your own heart and admit that there are true elements of selfishness that exist in there that need to be eradicated? Part of being a Christian is accepting that we are no longer lord of own lives anymore. We must submit to God and to whomever He puts in authority over our lives.

The ultimate example of Jesus's prayer in Luke 22:42 is how Jesus Himself lived it out. Jesus came to earth with the knowledge that His purpose was to be the Lamb of God who would lay down His life for the sins of the world. He prophesied it Himself throughout His earthly ministry. It was no surprise to Him that this was to be the end of the story.

But the night before His death was to take place, Jesus went to a favorite spot to pray and sought a different finale. "Must I die this way, isn't there another way we can save mankind? NOT MY WILL, BUT THY WILL BE DONE." Three times this was prayed, which indicates the great duress that was going on. Luke indicates that, as He prayed, Jesus sweat great drops of blood due to the blood vessels in His forehead popping as He prayed ever so intently with the weight of the man's eternity literally on His shoulders (Luke 22:44).

Jesus surrendered to His Father's perfect will and our salvation and secure eternity are the results. Incalculable good came out of such injustice and pain. Has God changed in what He requires of us or are we beginning to understand that this is God's modus operandi? He turns the most horrendous injustice into something gloriously praiseworthy. When Joseph was sold into slavery, his downward spiral was turned into the ladder of success and blessing. He coined a phrase for all time: "What you meant for evil, God devised a plan and turned it into something good – the salvation of our family" (Genesis 50:20). In the same way, Jesus' death and resurrection opened the door for us to come back into full relationship with our God and Father.

God is perfect in all His ways, perfect in His ability to bring great good out of great evil. Our responsibility is to submit to His will, which has always been for the good of His children.

*Lord, I submit to You, my life, my hopes, my dreams and my all. Not my will but Your will be done in me and through me to your praise and glory.*

## Day 38

## Joining the List of World Changers

**"The earth and everything in it, the world and all its inhabitants; belong to the Lord".** Psalm 24:1

I'm not sure where you are as you are reading this, but if you're in proximity to a window, please look outside. What do you see? A blue sky or clouds galore? Wind blowing through leaves on trees? Or is it winter, with a landscape of white? Maybe you are blessed to have a seascape and can hear the waves beating against the shore. Our God and King made this earth and He loves it but He made us to reign and rule on this earth in His stead. It is out of His love for us that He sent His Son to die in our place. God desires that His Kingdom come and His will be done on this planet that He created.

I've lived on three different continents and visited a fourth, as a child I always dreamed of traveling from place to place. God put a desire to do missionary work in Africa and in His time He fulfilled a portion of it. In the process He spoke to my heart that I would travel to other nations as well. Each time I board a plane to Minister God's word I am reminded how great God is that He is fulfilling His word to my heart. I find myself falling more and more in love with the people that He made and the earth that He created.

The beauty that surrounds us on earth is unsurpassed in the entire universe. Mountain tops and mountain lakes, savannahs and grasslands, gorges and grottos, deserts and seascapes, islands and arctic glaciers—all designed by the Master to enable us to marvel and glory at His greatness.

Mankind, with all of our idiosyncrasies, are the masterpieces that God created when He created this planet and placed us here. Jesus said in John 3:16, "For God so loved the world that He gave His only begotten Son." He also says through the Apostle Paul in Romans 8:21-23 that all creation groans in waiting for the manifestation of godly authority and rule in the earth. God does not love the world system and its carnal laws, but He does love everything that He placed on the earth and will, through His Church, bring it back to the glorious state before sin.

We have the awesome privilege to pray for earth and to see answers to our prayers take place because we prayed. We see examples of this throughout the Bible. Elijah was a man just like us who, through his prayers and obedience, changed the course of a nation's history. Esther and Mordecai were people cut from the same cloth as us and they made earth a better place to be because of their prayerfulness. Daniel was a man willing to lay down his life for his prayer times. He prayed for the revealed will of God through the prophets to take place. He was hated for his devotion and for his wisdom. His enemies laid a trap because of his devotion to God and he ended up in a den of starving lions. Daniel was honored by God when not one lion touched him for the duration of his stay. The king gave glory to God for this praying man.

Nations can still be impacted by a praying church. Harriet Beecher Stowe, a minister's daughter and a praying woman, declared that her book *Uncle Tom's Cabin* was a result of visions given to her by God. The book moved a nation to end the despicable practice of slavery.

The list of those who've prayed through to see God's will fulfilled in the earth is endless. Will you join the list?

Daddy, I gladly join the list of those praying and believing for YOU to come down and heal our lives. Let the fullness of YOUR will and YOUR Desires be fulfilled on the earth that you made for Holy purposes. Let everything that would stand in the way of YOUR perfect will be cast aside and broken to smithereens.

## Month Two

## The Believer's Communion

### Week One

1. What is it that great lovers do and how does this relate to our prayer life?
2. Religion makes slaves, God makes sons and daughters, and what does the Spirit cry inside of your heart to God?
3. If Jesus were on planet earth today what would he be doing?
4. What is God's modus operandi?
5. Pick a verse from week one and begin memorizing for next week.

## Day 39

## Heaven's Heartbeat

**"I know a man in Christ who was caught up into the heaven"** 2 Corinthians 12: 2

Ever been? To heaven I mean. Have you ever been to heaven? A couple Bible writers declare that they have been there or at least had a peek in. Moses, Elijah, Paul and John all give us testimonies of inside heaven. But what I want to say to you is this: every day that you enter His gates with thanksgiving and His courts with praise is a day in which we are invited into the very heart of heaven as we meet with God. It is also when and where we get recalibrated to know and understand what God's Kingdom and will are like.

If we consider how heaven must operate, we get a clearer and fuller picture of how earth was meant to operate from the beginning. Man's big problem begins with "I", the middle of sin and the middle of pride. Heaven, however, is devoid of pride and is instead a kingdom of servants.

Jesus is the King of Kings and the Lord of Lords, but He came as servant intent on meeting the needs of His subjects. Because Christ emptied Himself and was willing to be a humble servant all the days of His life, God released that great anointing on His life to minister powerfully throughout His earthly ministry. All that He did was for others, not for Himself: the sleepless prayer-filled nights, enduring rejection from His own people, the misunderstanding of His family, the priesthood who hated Him. His disciples not getting His message could have been enough for Him to throw in the towel! But Jesus persevered because His eyes were on the Father's plan and He knew it could not fail.

Jesus embodied the heartbeat of heaven, which is leading through serving. It is a leadership that is not focused on self but on others. True humility that knows how great one may be in Christ, but sets self aside in order to serve instead of seeking to be served. Jesus was due honor and glory beyond our wildest dreams, but He laid it all aside and humbled Himself to the most humiliating of deaths. When Peter rebuked Jesus for declaring He was destined for the cross, Jesus rebuked the source of the concern, saying, "Satan you are concerned with the issues of man; I am concerned with the issues of God. Get out of my way, Satan. I am going to the cross" (Matthew 16:13-23). Human nature is self-preserving. Only a selfless person would lay down their life for another.

If we do not understand the Kingdom of which we are a part, we can wrongly idolize human effort or gifting. God honors and exalts us when we humble and abase ourselves. Let us be honest; we so disapprove when someone gets the credit that we rightly deserve. I know of a man who had written a great book of spiritual revelation and insight that had taken years to study and prepare. A manuscript of his work was stolen from his home and published under another man's name. His attitude was, "I am so pleased that the body of Christ will be exposed to these truths". God has so blessed this man's life and ministry that the truths that God has revealed to him are blessing the body of Christ around the world.

If we do our part and mirror heaven's attitude, God will never fail to do His part.

*Pray as you feel led to.*

## Day 40

## Aligned Faith

**"Give us this day, our daily bread."** Matthew 6:11

How great is it to know that there is a God who cares so much that He calls us to ask Him for what we need each day.

God, in revealing His names to His people in the Old Testament, did so in such a way as to communicate that He was all that they would ever need. These are called the Jehovistic names of God. When God revealed Himself to Moses and said the ever famous "I AM THAT I AM" He was also implying – I AM everything that my people will ever need ME to be. When we look at Israel in the wilderness, we see the loving care of a God who met their needs even before they asked. The daytime heat was looked after by the cloud of God's presence. The cool nights were warmed by the pillar of fire (Exodus 13:21-22). God proved to the Israelites that He was the Great I AM by delivering them, healing them, feeding them, directing them, fighting for them, discipline them and nurturing them.

In Matthew 6:11, in the heart of Jesus' teaching on prayer, we hear the words, "Give us this day our daily bread". "*If God knows what we have need of before we ask Him, why ask?*" we may think. It is more for us than it will ever be for Him. It is not a duty; it is not a requirement; it is not to be religious. Our asking aligns our faith. We make it clear to God, to the enemy and to ourselves that we live in dependence on God. God is the perfect provider and the One that is pleased foremost when we come to Him in faith.

When my children come to me and ask me for food because they are hungry or for new shoes because theirs have worn out, do they have to go through a routine or rite of passage to ask? No way! They simply say, "Dad, did you do the shopping? I am hungry. What do we have to eat? Dad, my shoes are toast. I need new ones so I can play hoop." This is the normal order of things.

Jesus makes it crystal clear later on in the Sermon on the Mount that this is exactly how we should approach God the Father—not with ritual and religiosity, but with confidence and with faith in His abounding love and care for us. Your earthly father would not substitute a stone for bread or a snake for a fish; how dare you think that your heavenly Father would do less for your honest needs (Luke 11:11-13)? The heart of God is clearly revealed when Jesus says, "Come and ask Me." For why would He want you to ask if He did not intend to answer?

*Dad, it is so comforting to know that You have invited me into this divine love affair. I want to start with saying thank You for all that You have provided when I didn't even know it was You who was looking after me. I come with faith and an expectancy to see my daily needs furnished through Your grace.*

## Day 41

### "Forgive us our Sins"

**"And forgive us our debts as we forgive our debtors"** Matthew 6:12

Repentance is central to the issue of true salvation. One does not come and seek forgiveness if one is not convicted of sin and see the need to ask for forgiveness, which is the first step of repentance. Those who go through the motions of asking for forgiveness but never truly experience a change have not found true repentance. Saying, "I am sorry; please forgive me!" and *meaning* "I am sorry; please forgive me!" are two totally different things (Matthew 21:28-29).

The most precious gift you can have in life is a heart of repentance—seeing yourself for what you truly are without the grace and gift of salvation working in your life. The conflict over nature or nurture still rages in educational facilities, but more and more people are choosing to lean toward the idea that nurture is the only reason why any of us chooses to do wrong. Yet, I have never ever had to teach my children, to tell a lie, to hide the truth, to steal a cookie or to come right out and say "no". We live in a day where it is politically incorrect to explain life in terms of being born with a sinful nature. And yet, each and every one of us has been.

The revelation of one's own sinfulness is the doorway to the gift of salvation. I need a Savior who not only saves me for eternity, but who saves me now from my present sinfulness. When we come to God each day in earnest prayer, we come recognizing that in the last so many hours we may very well have sinned in one way or another. We need cleansing by the blood of the lamb and God makes it abundantly clear that cleansing is available (1 John 1:9).

Proverbs tells us to guard our heart for out of it flows all the issues of life (Proverbs 4:23). James tells us that God gives grace to the humble but He resists the proud (James 4:6). The proud usually end up that way from patting themselves on the back for their humility. "I am so humble" can be the first sound of a great, great fall. I will forever need a Saviour. I cannot save myself. My ability to keep short accounts with God ensures me of walking in His authority, His victory and His joy. My foremost desire should be to keep my slate clean before God, thus preventing any little sins in my life disrupting the flow of God's anointing in me and through me (Song of Solomon 2:15).

We are forgiven not because we are worthy, but because of His mercy and grace.

Psalm 51:7 says, "Purify me with hyssop, and I will be clean; wash me, and I will be whiter than snow."

*Pray as you feel led.*

## Day 42

### Forgiving Others

**"And be kind and compassionate to one another, forgiving one another, just as God also forgave you in Christ."** Ephesians 4:32

Today, we are going to continue with the theme of forgiveness. This one topic has in it the seeds of the greatest truths we can understand and incorporate into our lives. Our eternity hinges on whether or not we have been forgiven of all our sins. It is not what we have done or can do to merit His love and forgiveness; it is all about His loving grace and mercy that saves us. We have the easy part, believing that He died for us in our place. As we have given Him our sin, He has given us His righteousness. As we accept His blood sacrifice for us as sin offering, we are atoned for by His blood and are born again. We are sin free – that should make you want to jump and shout!

But now that we have been forgiven, do we forgive those who sin against us? There is an age-old statement that says, "To err is human, but to forgive is divine." Now, you may disagree with the statement or you may agree, but the point is that forgiveness mirrors a Christ-like nature and God hinges our own forgiveness with our ability to forgive others. In other words, if we do not give to others what has been given to us, than what has been given to us will be taken away.

The parable in Matthew 18:21-35 reiterates this principle for all of us. How can we who have been forgiven our great debt not forgive a debt incurred by someone else? The statement on the cross by Jesus has always been a source of refuge to me: "Father, forgive them for they do not know what they are doing." If I apply this to those who have sinned against me, it is so much easier to forgive them. In light of eternity, the cross, the judgment to come, my pain, their sin nature, their pain, and the work of the enemy behind the scenes, I choose to forgive and to be free.

A simple truth is that forgiving an offender is a gift we give to ourselves even more than a gift we give to the offender. This is true simply because we are the ones left in bondage when we do not forgive. We are the ones living with the torment of a past event. We are the ones unable to move on and get on with our lives, the ones who are seeing everything through a rear view mirror when our whole lives are before us. The person against whom we have a grudge has moved on, probably not even remembering the event that has crippled us beyond belief.

We can nail it to the cross and we can choose to leave it there and move on into what God has for us if we simply choose to. In choosing to forgive anyone of the debt that they owe us, the weight is lifted off of us and we are free to love and to live.

When we hold on to it we are weighted down by the grief and the pain of it and we find it impossible to move past it. God is so opposed to this way of living that He communicates to us, "Son, Daughter, I forgive you. Now you forgive. If you will not forgive those who have hurt you, then I withhold My forgiveness, for your sins against Me are far, far greater than any sin committed against you." The wondrous part of this is that He enables us to do it.

*Thank Him for that right now and forgive anyone who has wounded you.*

## Day 43

## Forgiving Yourself

**"He forgives all our sins......As far as the east is from the west, so far has He removedour transgressions from us."** Psalm 103:3a; 12 (Holman Christian Standard Bible)

I was fourteen at a youth camp and not even six months saved when a bunch of older boys invited me into their cabin for a drink. It was "sock hop" night and, although it was the 70's, we were having a 50's night dance. The drink I was being offered was not pop but something much stronger. I had never tasted alcohol before, but I made the mistake of having some with the guys that night. The next morning, the camp director called us three boys to his office. He was deeply grieved in his heart for us and gave us the opportunity to repent for what we had done. It was especially hard on me, as he made it crystal clear that I was the last person in the camp that he would have ever thought would participate in such an event.

We had to go back to our bunks for the morning and I found myself overwhelmed with condemnation and feelings of despair. A long list was paraded in my mind of how useless I was and of what a great failure I was now and would always be. I felt that I had so disappointed the director and my mom if she knew. And I thought about how upset God must be with me for this work of my flesh. As I writhed on this bed in emotional pain and spiritual attack, a still small Voice spoke to my heart, "Stephen, do you forgive yourself for what you have done?" I pondered this for a couple of minutes. I had never heard of this before and, being newly saved, had never heard a message on it either. I prayed and asked God to help me understand what He was saying to my heart. "If I forgave you and tossed your sin away, if I refuse to bring it up again and if I refuse to remember it ever happened, should you continue in this self-loathing that I died to remove from your life?"

I quickly forgave myself and immediately my joy returned. I was back on cloud nine, loving God and praising Him for His goodness to me. I ran into the other boys who were walking around dejected, depressed, condemned and joyless. I told them what the Lord said to me and was offering them, but they choose to stay in their condemned state.

So what about you? What will you do when you sin in a way that you think you never will? Maybe you already have. Now is the time to incorporate into your heart that when God forgives you, He also expects you to forgive yourself. There is no penance in the Bible and there is nothing you can do to save yourself. We do not add to the work of the cross to get God's forgiveness. From God's perspective that is what we do when we emotionally flagellate ourselves by allowing the enemy to tell us how wicked and sinful we are. When we have asked for forgiveness and truly repented, we are restored to right relationship to God with no mark against us. Who are we to add to the cross of Christ? The price He paid was more than enough; nothing can be added to it. He alone saves, not the cross and penance, not the cross and good works, and not the cross and condemnation. Forgive yourself and let it go.

*Daddy, I accept what Jesus has done for me. I forgive myself for my sins as well and I take the fullness of Your grace into my heart and walk in Your loving acceptance.*

## Day 44

## A Life of Overcoming

**"And do not bring us into temptation"** Matthew 6:13a

Life is filled with tests, trials and temptations. We are tempted, James 1:14-15 says, based on what is in our hearts. If certain sins are not in our hearts, they will not be a temptation to us. But if they are in our hearts, then the battle to see whether we will overcome or give in begins. Paul tells us in 1 Corinthians 10:13 that all temptation is common and ordinary for man, but God is faithful who will not allow us to be tempted above what we are able. I believe Jesus' teaching on prayer is interwoven with this understanding. What good would it be to any of us if inherent in every temptation was the assurance of failure? Thankfully, within every temptation God gives us the promise of victory.

I have three children in school. My eldest is about to graduate and they are in a school that insists on honors. They fail if they don't get 80%. To them, that has become their 50% and so their standard is automatically raised as to what they must achieve. Now if the tests were written in such a way that guaranteed the failure of the students, it would not be long before we would have a full scale revolt on our hands. Yes, I know at times our children try to convince us that the test is rigged and no one could ever pass it. God has not jury-rigged life so that we come out with the short end of the stick. No, He promises to always lead us in joyful procession or in overwhelming victory (2 Corinthians 2:14).

When we follow God's lead, we will always be led to victory. When we take the lead and follow our senses, our desires, our will, what society dictates and so on and so forth, we end up in sin or defeat. Victory is ours, it is a free gift and we wake up every morning in victory. We choose to keep it as the day proceeds or to give it away. God will lead us and guide us all the way. If we stay obedient and trusting, we will see daily victories turn into a life of overcoming.

Determine in your heart that you are going to follow the lead of Jesus example, that you will listen to the inner voice of the Holy Spirit directing your path and that the authority of God's word over your life will always be without question. If you follow these three truths you will always overcome the enemy.

Daddy, I am so grateful that YOU will never give me more than I can handle. That You will always be with me to strengthen me to defeat the work of hell in my life. The question will come down to who will align my will with, with You and Your truths or with my flesh or hell's lies.

## Day 45

### Eyes To See

**"But deliver us from the evil one"** Matthew 6:13b

Here is the opposite side to yesterday's message. Though God will never lead us in over our heads, there is an adversary who delights in trying to do just that. The enemy of our souls has one trick left up his sleeve that he successfully employs against the sons of Adam and the daughters of Eve – deception. Jesus, on the cross, stripped Satan of all his power and authority over us. (Colossians 2:15)

Satan is a lion seeking who he may devour, but he is toothless. In place of what he had, he has consorted to his original bag of tricks which he employed in the garden. In the garden, when man was first made, Satan showed up in the form of a serpent and deceived Adam and Eve with his words.

When God showed up on the scene there was no confrontation between the devil and God. During the entire discussion between God and His children, Satan offered no two cents whatsoever. He remained silent during the entire exchange. When Adam and Eve have finished their blame shifting, God brought judgment and he started with the devil. The devil was powerless to offer any resistance whatsoever. He did not call his thousands of demons to assault God or to try and overthrow heaven. God pronounced His judgment on the enemy and it was done. No battle, no fight, no resistance. God spoke and it was enacted.

Jesus came to earth as the second Adam to begin His earthly ministry. After baptism, the Spirit of God led Him into a forty day fast in a wilderness where He was to be tempted and tested. (Remember yesterday, to a battle that He was able to win). Satan showed up and three times tried to get Jesus to sin, just once. Each time, Jesus deflected the lie with the truth of the Word of God. Lucifer was defeated again with the power of God's Word over his deceptive lies. No battle, no fight, no resistance. God's Word was remembered, spoken and enacted.

Three and a half years later, Satan, not knowing He was a pawn in the Father's hand, entered Judas, who betrayed Christ to be captured and crucified. This time it looked like a literal fight would erupt. Jesus declared that He could call twelve legions of angels to rescue Him but instead, like a lamb to the slaughter, He died on the cross. It might appear that the victor on that day was the enemy, but in fact, what looked like victory was the greatest defeat possible. For Jesus stripped Satan of all his authority and power and symbolically took the keys of rulership from him and gave them back to man. No battle, no fight, no resistance. Jesus died and enacted new life for all of us to enjoy.

My simple purpose in sharing these thoughts is to show what we already know: there is no battle between God and the enemy. The lie of the day of a balance of power in the force, yin and yang, good versus evil are false concepts that allow us to think that somehow Lucifer has a chance. His defeat is without doubt. It is our job to show how great our God is over the enemy. The prayer for deliverance over the evil one is for us to recognize that the enemy is still working to deceive, to twist and turn the truth of God's Word and to cause us to doubt or misunderstand what God has spoken. We pray for eyes to see the truth of the Word of who we are in Him and our rightful authority over all the works of the devil.

*Thank You, oh God, that I am victorious in You and that the enemy of my soul has been clearly defeated, disarmed and disabled by Your great power. I am able to live victoriously and triumphantly, able to be an overcomer. Deliver me from all of the enemy's wicked schemes and traps. Help me to see them for what they are and to follow You whole-heartedly to bring others out of His lies and deception.*

## Week Two

1. Forgiving others can many times be easier than forgiving ourselves; do you need to forgive yourself of something permanently? Do it now and let the joy of the Lord fill your heart completely.
2. What is inherent in every temptation?
3. What qualifies us for re-commissioning? Rightly responding to God gives us a promise for what in our future?
4. God uses ordinary everyday people to do extraordinary miracles, how does this happen?
5. Quote your verse from last week and pick a meaningful verse for next week to begin working on.

## Day 46

## Purification Before Advancement

**Read Isaiah 6:1-8**

Isaiah is a prophet who has come before God to worship and pray while his nation is in a time of mourning and transition. A righteous King has died and the man of God is in prayer. A great vision from God begins to unfold before Isaiah, only he is not reading it, he is experiencing it. Upon the revelation of God's holiness, Isaiah proclaims, "Doom! It's Doomsday! I'm as good as dead! Every word I've ever spoken is tainted—blasphemous even! For my eyes have seen the King, the Lord of Angel Armies." Isaiah comes into a full view of his own sinfulness when he is confronted with God's glory.

The very first stage of any true visitation of God is an acknowledgement of God's holiness and our sinfulness. We are great in our own eyes or when we compare ourselves to someone else, but when we have a clear revelation of who God is, then and only then do we realize we are all in the same boat. We are sinners in need of grace before a holy and righteous God.

Isaiah's declaration of God's purity and of the seraphim around him confirm that God visited him in might and power. God heard Isaiah's cry and immediately responded. An angel was sent to take a burning coal off of an altar and to press it to Isaiah's lips. Upon touching his lips, the angel declares, "Gone your guilt, your sin is wiped out." How transformative is this picture of how immediate heaven responds. As soon as Isaiah acknowledged his sinfulness God responded to remove the obstacle. God did not sugar coat it and say it was not there, but immediately did something about it.

In this picture, Isaiah's sin is not covered over with blood, but instead it is actually burnt away. When something is burnt, it is changed forever. It doesn't matter what it is, when something passes through fire, the fire changes the very essence of the thing. The picture here is one of a changed nature, a foretaste of what God would do through Christ on the cross. Isaiah saw his need to be a greater instrument for God. He saw the desperate state of the nation and sought God as the only source of help. But in the process of seeking God, God was seeking Isaiah, to take him to another level of usefulness. But before He could advance him, He had to purify him so that he could have a greater ministry and influence.

Sixty more chapters await Isaiah, but I don't believe for a second they would have borne his name if he had not allowed God to fully purify His lips so that he could be a mouthpiece for God.

*My heart cries out, "Here I am, send me!" But I understand that for each yes, there is a price of purity that is required. Daddy, I am learning that Your love is perfect towards me and You will provide the grace I need to be purified. All the glory goes to You and so I say, "Have Your way."*

## Day 47

### Who Will Go For Us

**'And then I heard the voice of the Master: "Whom shall I send? Who will go for us?" I spoke up, "I'll go. Send me!'** Isaiah 6:8

The Word of God reveals to us the relationship between God and His creation. It show us live and in technicolor what a relationship with God looks like. In other words, we should be able to look at our lives and experiences with God and see them mirrored in the Word of God. It is an intimate, personal book that pictures for us the experiences that we are to have in our lives as well.

Isaiah 6 opens with the death of a righteous king. Transitional times are always challenging and difficult times. Whenever there is a crisis in life we need to go to our true source of strength and comfort. Israel had a long history of unrighteous and evil kings. Now a righteous king had just died and the incumbent king gave little indication that He would be righteous as his father. Isaiah went to God and saw the true King of Israel, the true majesty and potentate. Isaiah fixes his eyes on God and knows that no matter what life circumstances hold, God is still on the throne and rules and reigns in all of life's affairs. Much transpires here and just as the revelation is fading, Isaiah hears God ask – who will go for us, who can we send – Isaiah responds – Here I am, send me.

Prayer has always been designed to be revelatory. God seeks a people in and through whom He can reveal more and more of Himself:

> I am calling to you. I know you by name. I made you for Myself. I know your past, your present and your future, for I hold them in the palm of My hand. I call you to My service as an instrument in My Hand that I can wield as I choose. For I have a work that only you can do, the gifts and the talents that I have endowed you with are for My purposes and plans that My kingdom may be extended. Expect great and glorious events to transpire in your life and through your life because I am with you to empower you, strengthen you and to bless you.

This is what God is speaking at the very center of His call for one who would go and be a representation of His will and purpose.

In Isaiah 6:8, the heart of God's people is emulated in the cry of Isaiah. When I picture this event in my mind's eye and God asks the question, "Whom shall I send and who will go for us?" I see Isaiah jumping and waving His hands and yelling at the top of lungs, "Here I am! Send me! Send me! Send me!" His heart was yearning and longing to be used by God. He had just been cleansed and now came the re-commissioning call.

God does not only call us once, but as we are transformed and changed, cleansed and revived, He calls us up with a higher call and a greater revelation of Himself to do more for Him than we could have done before. In John 15:16, Jesus called it "pruning" and reiterates the call.

Isaiah was already a useful prophet when God re-commissioned Him in Isaiah 6. How do we know that the book of Isaiah would have been 5 chapters instead of 66 if He had not allowed God to do the inner cleansing work that was required in Him so that he could move into all that God had for Him? Isaiah's repentance qualified him for re-commissioning. Without his repentance and humility, he would never have heard the call to go for God. His right response to God positioned Him for the more that God had for Him to do.

Respond to the call of God upon your life.

*God, I say "Here am I. Send me! Use me for your Glory! Fill me with more of You! Overflow me, purify me and use me as a vessel in Your Hand.*

## Day 48

### When is Similarity Good?

**"Elijah was a human being with a nature such as we have [with feelings, affections, and a constitution like ours]; and he prayed earnestly for it not to rain, and no rain fell on the earth for three years and six months. [18] And [then] he prayed again and the heavens supplied rain and the land produced its crops [as usual]"** James 5:17 (Amplified Bible)

A great man of God named K.R. Iverson commented that there a two things that hinder God's Spirit from being poured out as He should be making the church the effective agent in the earth.—"I have seen two things that inhibit the release of the lifestyle God wants in the Church. First, the deifying of ministry positions and secondly, the deifying of the gifts." 8 In many ways, we are little different from the world in that we have our own Christian Hollywood in the way that we treat those behind the pulpit.

Moses declared, "Oh that all God's people were prophets!" Numbers 11:29 Elijah and Moses were the two prophets that visited Jesus on top of the Mount of Transfiguration – and we have them on pretty lofty pedestals. It is no wonder that Peter said, "It would be good for us to build three tabernacles here." Matthew 17:4 We get a glimpse into a mindset that most of us share. We exalt the servants of God as almost equal to God. On the Mount of Transfiguration, the cloud of the Father's presence came and said, "This is my beloved Son. Hear Him." Elijah and Moses were echoes of the Son. They prefigured Him and prepared us for Him, but they are not Him and so should not be treated as He should be treated. Human nature likes to see what it is worshipping and we see around the world today worship of images and of people. What most of us do not realize is that because we were created to worship we will always find something or someone to worship. Satan has always readily provided an idol to worship along with a snare.

In James 5:17, it is as though God is saying, "I want more Elijah's. Please understand that he was just like you. He was fallible, flawed, felt what you feel and yet when he prayed, I listened and shut the heavens for three and a half years." We have to take our religious tinted glasses off and understand that God uses ordinary, everyday people to do extraordinary miracles, not because of who they are, but because of who He is.

The Pharisees took note that the disciples who did miracles had been with Jesus (Acts 4:13). Elijah's ministry was noted by signs and wonders, as was his successor Elisha, who doubled his miraculous output. God wants to raise up a great army of believers who are not impressed with the titles and positions of man, but who are clearly focused on *Jesus* and extending His kingdom with signs and wonders, which are the normal outflow of God's Kingdom and presence in the earth.

Testimonies are increasing from all the nations of the earth of the outpouring of God's Spirit. Wherever you are and whatever situation you are in, the God of miracles is alive, present and willing to do miracles that would exalt His *name* and draw people to Him. Be a person who prays expecting and believing for miracles. It should be the norm for the church, not the exception.

*Yes, Lord, my heart says yes to Your will and yes to Your ways. Use Your Church to reveal Your power and Your glory in the earth.*

8. Iverson, Dick & Asplund, (1995) Building Churches That Last. Portland, Oregon : Bible Temple Publications

## Day 49

### Persistence in Prayer

**Read Luke 18:1-8**

God is always looking for faith. It is somewhat amazing that Christ should ask, "Will I find faith on the earth?" How would you answer that question? I don't believe it is rhetorical, but was instead a way in which God is stirring our hearts to respond with a glorious, “Yes, Lord, You will find faith on the earth when you come. I will have faith Lord. Help me to have faith.”

The greatest battles that you will ever face in your life will always be concerning whether or not you will believe God and take Him at His Word. It is that plain and that simple-- so simple that a child can understand—and that is why it is so hard for us. When we pray for the Kingdom of God to come and the will of God to be done in earth as it is in heaven, the answer to that prayer is going to rock the gates of hell and bring souls rushing into the kingdom of heaven. Satan is not going to stand by and applaud such Holy Ghost prayers and so, before such prayers can be prayed, he sows doubt, questions, problems and issues to prevent the thing that he fears the most—faith filled persistent prayer. It only goes to reason that if God loves faith-filled persistent praying, then Satan would hate it and fight it more than any other thing. Is it any wonder that prayer meetings are the most least attended meetings in churches unless those churches are on fire?

Thayer’s Greek Dictionary defines the word Jesus uses in regard to fainting- as to be utterly spiritless, to be wearied out, and exhausted.9 This speaks volumes as to what we must guard against in our prayer lives. The question I like to ask myself is this: I want to pray the things that have eternal significance, that will bring glory to God and that will produce supernatural events in my life and time. God loves persistence and therefore if I am going to pray for such things and I know they are God’s heart than I cannot give up until God gives me peace that the time is now. Now I can just praise and thank HIM for the answers that are coming. In my own strength I will get wearied, exhausted and hopeless, but as I persist in faith and not be weary victory in prayer precedes victory in our circumstances.

“I am looking for those who will persist in prayer for what they know is My heart and My will. Those who will weather the storms of delay, lies of denial, feelings of rejection and thoughts of abandonment. Those who will persist despite the difficulty and who will quote My Word back to me, in faith and in trust, declaring, 'I know You will do it, for You are faithful to every promise. It is just a matter of time, Your perfect time.'"

*Yes Lord, Yes Lord, I will learn to pray just like that. Yes Lord, pour out Your Spirit over all the earth as You promised You would.*

9. Strong's Nt 1590 Thayer's Greek Lexicon, Electronic Database – Copyright © 2002, 2003, 2006, 2011 by Bible Soft Inc. All Rights Reserved. Used by Permission

## Day 50

### The Cry of Submission

**Going a little farther, He fell facedown and prayed, "My Father! If it is possible, let this cup pass from Me. Yet not as I will, but as You will."** Matthew 26:39

The night of Jesus' betrayal, Jesus met with His Father in the Garden of Gethsemane. The book of John records the high priestly prayer of Jesus as He prays for His disciples and He prays for us (John 17). His heart is on others before it is on Himself. He considers us and how we will walk in His truth and receive His glory. But, as the time passes and the reality of tomorrow sets in, Jesus must get away and so He goes to a favorite spot, a garden. It is a garden similar to where man was first placed and, there, Jesus engages in a battle not seen with human eyes, a battle of the soul and of the will. Will I go to the cross or not? He petitions His Father and asks if there is another way the salvation of man can be accomplished. The foundation of this prayer and all of Jesus' praying was "Not My will, But Thy will be done".

Consider for a moment the greatness of this struggle. God the Son is about to become sin. He has enjoyed perfect communion with God the Father and God the Holy Spirit from eternity past. Sin has always been the one thing that God hates more than anything else in the universe. Yet, the thing that God hates so much, the Son is not only going to carry, but He is going to *become*.

Jesus is weighing the extent of this. Being fully God, He knows how the Godhead feels about sin. We know that, on the cross, Jesus cries out and says, "My God, My God, why have you forsaken me?" Matthew 27:45 although it was a fulfillment of scripture, it was also an actual cry, an actual experience that caused such a cry to come out.

Somewhere in the moment, whether your theology agrees that the Father turned away or not, Isaiah 53 makes it crystal clear the Father dumped all of His wrath meant for sin upon His Son. There was a disruption of fellowship and communion between the Godhead on the cross and Jesus, foreseeing it in the garden, sweats great drops of blood as He considers the price that He, the perfect Son, the suffering servant, has to fully choose in time what He had chosen in eternity past, to become the blood sacrifice for you and for me. To know a millisecond of separation that we might never, never, ever experience it in time or in eternity.

King Jesus is perfect in every aspect. Prayer is not just communion; it is an expression of His person—submitted, humble, and self-controlled. Again, the cry comes forth from His essence, "Not My will, but Thy will be done." It is clear that one will trumps the other will. The Father's will is perfect for each and every one of us.

Here before us is the living testimony of every prayer that we will ever pray. When we live in surrender to God's will, His character and nature in us reveals to us the mind and heart of God. Prayer becomes an outward expression of an inward Holy Spirit conviction of what God desires. Once we discover the will of God, prayer becomes easier and easier, more Spirit led and Word-confirmed as we pray in the very will of God. Praying for miracles or miraculous intervention doesn't seem too hard to pray, for Jesus did it all the time. If we are following His example than should that not be ordinary Christian praying? We will save that for another time.

*Papa, oh for the heart that continually cries, "Not my will but Your will be accomplished." The more I see who You are, the more I desire to be a conduit of Your perfect will. Help me to be like Jesus, the perfect expression of who you are and what You desire. Help me to mirror that each and every day.*

## Day 51

### The Cry of Submission (Part 2)

**"Going a little farther, He fell facedown and prayed, "My Father! If it is possible, let this cup pass from Me. Yet not as I will, but as You will."** Matthew 26:39

One of the eye-opening moments of my Christian experience was to realize how central and significant my will is to God and to my living a life in the very center of His will, saying what He would say and doing what He would do. Every step forward in life is based on the choices we make. Submitting our will is the first step to the greatness that God wants to release in our lives.

Our will is connected to our speech. When Jesus prayed, He declared aloud for all heaven and earth to hear, "Father, I am submitted to You. I will do what You ask Me to do, not what I want or desire or feel that I need. I set my will to do Your will. Ask and I will obey."

Throughout the Word of God, we are confronted with declarations of praise and of worship and of determinations to do what is good and right. For example, David declared time and time again, "I will bless the Lord, I will praise Your name forever. With my mouth I will make known Your faithfulness." Over and over and over again, the will is set to do what is right and pleasing to God. The choice is not made because it is easy, but because it is right and when we set our will to do what is right, the right will always get accomplished. That is the intrinsic power of the will. When it is submitted to God, great miracles will be done.

Galatians tells us that we are crucified in Christ, yet we live. Our sin nature has been put to death. The power of sin to control us and bring sin into our life has been broken by our death in Christ (Galatians 2:20). We have been purchased and we are to be a love-slave. Our life is not our own. We have been purchased with a price and we are to be a living sacrifice, always upon God's altar. We know that Isaac got up of off the altar of sacrifice, but Christ did not. We live by a new power and with a new nature. The nature of Christ has been given to us. It is the truest evidence of our new birth. We hunger for spiritual truth more than for natural food. We are famished for the Word of God, for it is our strength and nourishment. We are no longer self-centered and selfishly oriented. We place God's will and ways first. We work to see God's will accomplished in the earth more than our own.

All men and women of God who submit to God's will and qualify to be used by God find themselves in the awesome place of being used mightily by God. Jesus was the prototype man. He showed us how God would interact in and through a man who was in total submission to His will, a man living in victory over sin and one who was filled to overflowing with love for others ahead of love for self. God has not changed. He is still looking for the same kind of men and women. When we respond like Jesus, we will see the same power and glory revealed, because He has opened the heavens for us.

Daddy, thank you so much for YOUR patience and longsuffering with me, I can only imagine how YOU long for us to submit to YOUR ways so that we can experience the joy and fulfillment YOU always intended for us. The taste of YOUR glory that I have experienced through submitting produces a hunger in me to run hard after YOU knowing I will always be outdone by YOUR love.

## Day 52

### The Cry For Presence

**"After this, when Jesus knew that everything was now accomplished that the Scripture might be fulfilled, He said, "I'm thirsty!"** John 19:28

The words of Jesus ringing out from the cross cause one to ask the question: What in fact was Jesus thirsty for? He received the sour wine that was there and quickly declared that all was complete and died. If he had truly been thirsty for something of this earth or, in particular, water to quench His thirst, I believe he would have realized at that point that nothing natural could have been of benefit to him.

Jesus was thirsting not for medicine or for relief but for the only thing that can truly satisfy man in every state of our existence. He was thirsting for the very presence of His Father alone. The number of scriptures that allude to our spiritual hunger and thirst for God are a clear indication of this deeper cry within the child of God.

Moses put it in simpler terms, "If You're not coming with us than we are not going anywhere" (Exodus 33:14-15). The presence of God is the primary need in the life of all of humanity. The absence of the presence of God is hell. When you really take hell and heaven down to their singular difference, it is that one has the presence of God and one does not.

What makes heaven? Heaven is the presence of God, not the gold, precious stones, lighted city, big feast or lack of death or sorrow. These are all good things, but they would never satisfy or satiate an eternal being. *Nothing* can satisfy who we are! Only a *Person* can eternally fulfill us and that Person is our Source, our Maker, our Lover and our King who imbues us with significance.

Once we have seen Him and know that we were created to be like Him and then to be rejected by Him, that is hell indeed. The truest sense of hell is the absence of God. Jesus' teaching makes it quite clear that in hell there will be a great separation between those in judgment and those in blessing for eternity. Hell is described as a place where the worm never dies and a place of weeping and gnashing of teeth (Isaiah 66:24; Matthew 13:42 50). It is a place of eternal regret, remorse and unfulfilled desire. An eternal soul that can never have any needs met, but exists in the pain of unmet desires for eternity.

Jesus has become sin for us on the cross, He has declared that He feels forsaken of God and yet He is in the perfect will of God doing exactly what God would have him do. He thirsts not for what man can give, but what His Father alone can give. He is longing for the full communion and the eternal oneness with the Father and the Holy Spirit that He laid down for us.

*Daddy, there are so many people who have no idea of the joy and fulfillment that comes from knowing You. I thirst for more of You. You have satisfied and fulfilled my heart, but I long for more of You in my life. You have promised that as I draw near to You, You will draw near to me and so I come to You now.*

Week Three

1. What is the primary need in the life of all humanity?
2. God said yes to Moses request to see what? If God was willing to do it for Moses in the covenant of Law what is God willing to do in the Covenant of Grace?
3. Before God could advance Isaiah, He had to ........?
4. What initiates intercession?
5. Memory Work

## Day 53

### The Cry of Victory

### "It is Finished"

**When Jesus had received the sour wine, He said, "It is finished!" Then bowing His head, He gave up His spirit.** John 19:30

It goes without saying that cheaters never prosper and it would be equally true to say that quitters never prosper as well. The greater a godly vision, the greater the opposition will be for that vision to be accomplished. Consider for a moment that in the Garden of Gethsemane, 18 hours earlier Jesus was asking if there was another way to accomplish the task before Him that God would grant it. Jesus submitted to the Father's plan. The struggle He endured was because the price He was to pay was the greatest price that could be paid.

Everything was working against Him to throw in the towel, so that He would not endure. But He did endure the rejection, the torture, the cruelty, the hatred, the beating, the cat of nine tails and the imposition of sin upon His person. He had lived the life so that He could be the sinless sacrifice on our behalf. Only Christ could die for you and for me, because only His blood was sinless, enabling our life to be exchanged for His life. Now, God looks down and declares us righteous and sinless because we have been crucified with Christ and we live a new life as Christ lives through us (Romans 6).

Jesus declares from the cross that the plan of salvation, the price for salvation, has been accomplished, fulfilled. Thayer's word studies has as one of its definitions of this word – to perform the last act which completes a process.[10] Everything that needed to be done so that we could be saved, delivered and healed legally was fulfilled. There is no more judgment against us, no more condemnation, no more list of offences and transgressions. All of our failures, all of our sins and every righteous requirement that we've failed to meet has been nailed to the cross and removed (Colossians 2:14). Satan, the accuser of the brethren, does not have a leg to stand on when he comes to accuse us.

The Old Testament equivalent to what I am sharing is found in Zachariah 3 in which God will not allow Satan to accuse his servant – JOSHUA. – but his filthy garments which represent his sin and uncleanness before God, are removed and in their place a kingly robe is given and the crown of a High Priest is put upon his head. The Lord Himself rebukes Satan and his feeble attempt to castigate the servants of the Lord. (Zech. 3:1-7)

Finished, accomplished, done–now it is time for our hearts to praise and worship at what God has inaugurated on our behalf. There is not a mark against us. King Jesus completed the task for which He came and all of history and all of eternity are marked by the glory of the event that transformed our lives. Our prayer lives must be marked with the completed work of the cross. Heaven is open to us. The veil has been removed. There is open access because of the open heart of God. The ripped veil from the top to the bottom is God declaring that the sacrifice of His Son is accepted and now we have immediate entry into the immediate presence of God. It is just a prayer time away.

*God, I bless You; God I Praise You; God I thank You.*

10. Thayer and Smith. "Greek Lexicon entry for Teleo". "The NAS New Testament Greek Lexicon". . 1999.

## Day 54

## The Cry for Glory

**Read Exodus 33:18 - 23**

Throughout scripture, there is a continual hunger and thirst that comes from God's people to see God's glory and to know Him more. One of the great examples of this is before us today. Moses' heart cry should be our heart cry. This was during Old Testament Times; this was pre-cross; this was pre-Holy Spirit indwelling; this was before the Blood of Jesus made a way and before the veil of heaven was rent to allow us access into the Holy of Holies in the spirit and for eternity.

The awesome nature of the request is to be awed and echoed, but it is the response that we must take note of. God could have simply explained that what He sought could not be accomplished. He was not under any obligation to answer Moses' request and yet He did. For all the prophetic pictures and spiritual allegories that we can draw from this, the greatest truth of all must not be missed. God said yes. He showed Moses so much that Moses' face shone for weeks or months (2 Corinthians 3:7-18).

God wanted to be seen and He wanted to be known. He did not and He does not desire to be unknown to us. The more of Him we have, the more like Him we can be. We must consider that these are New Testament times and that we are in a different spiritual era than Moses was in.

My point is quite simple. God still desires to show His glory to His people. Jesus prayed it in the garden. He said that the Father had already given us the same glory that He had given His Son and that we might be where Jesus is so that we might behold His glory. Jesus' high priestly prayer is filled with the concept of glory being revealed. There is a greater glory revealed now in Christ than in any other spiritual epoch. The glory of the latter house is to be greater than the glory of the former house. We should be anticipating more, not less, of God's power and glory being revealed in us and through us.

Glory can be defined as a manifestation of God's power and beauty so intense and awesome that the only response we can give is to give honor, praise, worship and glory to God for what He has done. All who are present in a manifestation of God's glory will respond with glorifying the God who would do such an awesome miracle, healing, sign, wonder, deliverance, salvation, provision or pulling back the scales from our eyes and seeing Him in a supernatural revelation.

This should be the norm for the church, when we consider that the God of the Bible did miracles for His people continually and promised He would for us. We should be concerned when there are no miracles, no signs and no wonders. It would be a true indication that something is amiss. Not having the power of God flowing in our lives and ministry should be the most alarming aspect of our lives. Too many of us have settled for a powerless Christianity when God has made the way for us to experience His presence and authority in our lives.

What are you going to do about it?

*More Glory Lord, More Glory. I pray that You would reveal more of You through me. God, let Your glory be revealed in my life by drawing the lost to You. I want to be a shining testimony of who You truly are. Help me.*

## Day 55

## God's Love Initiates Intercession

**Read Genesis 18: 17-33**

I do not believe there is a more accurate picture of intercessory prayer than the scripture that we have before us today. Through covenant, God made a way for Abraham to be God's friend. God interacts with Abraham as an actual friend and confidant. God asks Himself, "Shall I hide from Abraham the things that I am about to do?" He then tells himself, "No, I will reveal it to him for I know him and I know how He will raise his children before me (Genesis 18:17, 18).

God's love initiates intercession and it is because of His great love for us and for those we will intercede for. True intercession cannot be faked. It flows from the Spirit of God in love for those who are perishing out of a heart that is filled with compassion. If we take a minute and compare Abraham and Jonah, we can see a marked difference between how these two men approached the news that judgment was coming to destroy a city.

Jonah was more than willing to see a city of millions wiped out by the judgment of God. He ran in disobedience because he did not want to see God show mercy to the city. The greatest revival recorded in scripture is given by a reluctant and angry prophet. But the response of the people is immediate. The people cried out to God for mercy and God heard and answered. Jonah became angry and told God how he knew this is what the outcome would be. He hung around to confirm that mercy came instead of judgment. God had a very powerful way of communicating to Jonah that his heart was not in unity with the heart of God. (Read the book of Jonah.)

Abraham's response over a far greater debauched people was immediate and God-like, compassionate, loving, caring and nurturing. Abraham humbled himself and challenged God to look at His own character: "Must not the judge of the whole earth, judge right?" Genesis 18:25 In this pre-law era, Abraham recognized that God as judge of the whole earth was still responsible to be perfect. Abraham discovered that God was willing to spare Sodom and Gomorrah if there were but ten righteous people. God could not find ten and the one He did find proved to be one who had some prominent moral confusion. But the picture given to us from this example from Abraham's life is that, although it appears every plan of God is already determined, God responds to prayer. Although He ultimately knows what He will do, He invites us into process of moving His heart right to where He knew it would be.

Just to be thought of as a friend of God should be mind boggling to us.

Great Lover of my soul, I take comfort in the fact that YOU are just and merciful. YOU have made a way for us to come back to YOUR very heart. For the many who do not know YOUR heart my prayer is that the scales would be removed from their eyes, their ears would be unplugged and every work of hell working against them would be utterly and completely destroyed and salvation, healing and wholeness would flow into and through their lives…….

## Day 56

## Intercession

**"First of all, then, I urge that petitions, prayers, intercessions, and thanksgivings be made for everyone"** I Timothy 2:1

The heart of intercession is the love of God. We intercede because, whether we know it or not, someone was interceding for us before we came to salvation. It may have been a parent, a neighbor, a friend, a relative, or a grandparent who may be dead and gone, but their intercessory prayer lives on in heaven and God, who heard and gave a promise, is now fulfilling His promise by beckoning you and me to Himself.

It thrills my soul to know that prayers are timeless. They affect generations and they change the course of nations, all because we take the time to pray for heaven to invade earth. God's love is what compels a person to develop a lifestyle of intercessory prayer. The more of God's love you have, the more you will be compelled to give that love away, the more your heart will break for others to know that love the more you will desire to help others find the joy and fulfillment that comes from co-labouring with God to reconcile others to Christ.

In intercession, you never have to wonder if you are praying the will of God, for scripture clearly reveals that God's will is that none should perish, but instead that all should come to saving grace (2 Peter 3:9). This means that all of the resources of heaven are at our disposal see those that we are praying for come to salvation.

D.L. Moody had a friend who was unsaved that he interceded for his entire life. Though God answered many, many prayers of Moody, this friend somehow seemed to elude coming to Christ. Moody passed away and never did see this friend get saved. But at his funeral, the gentleman was so wonderfully moved upon by the power of the Holy Spirit that he gave his life to Christ. Moody never saw him actually pray the prayer and his life be changed, but in his praying he most certainly did. Intercession believes it, claims it, declares it and receives it long before it happens in the natural.

My mother prayed for my siblings to come to Christ. It was her foremost prayer and desire but she went home to glory not seeing the fulfillment of this prayer. My sister, upon reading a letter addressed to an evangelist asking for prayer for her and our brother, found herself crying out to God for salvation. God took the very cry for more intercession to be the tool that He would use to reconcile a loved one back to Himself. How awesome is God in all of His works.

The good news of God's love is the greatest news in the world. An intercessor paves the way through prayer and readies hearts and minds to receive Christ.

*Daddy, there are many people in my life that do not know You for who are. Not only do I want to be a laborer in your harvest, I want to break the spiritual chains from their lives so they can hear the message when it is preached to them. Let me burn with a fire of love that fuels my times of prayer with You and my mouth with insight from You.*

**Day 57**

**The Greatest Attitude Adjuster**

**"Enter His gates with Thanksgiving and His courts with praise" Psalm** 100:4

**"Don't worry about anything, but in everything, through prayer and petition with thanksgiving, let your requests be made known to God. [7] And the peace of God, which surpasses every thought, will guard your hearts and minds in Christ Jesus."** Philippians 4:6

I don't know about you, but I enjoy a good old western movie every now and again. I don't really know what it is about them that makes me enjoy them so much, but it is a genre that I know a lot of people miss seeing. One thing that you find in most authentic westerns is the town salesman who has the most interesting gadgets and gizmos to help you with your everyday responsibilities, especially the lady of the house (not that different from modern day commercials). One common item for sale was the "cure all". It didn't matter what the disease, what the symptoms, how long you had it or whether it was fatal or not, if you took this "ointment", you would be cured. The idea of a "cure all" has seen its day. Or has it? I want to present to you the greatest attitude adjuster known to man – a heart of thanksgiving and gratitude.

Earlier in Philippians 2, Paul warns us against grumbling, complaining, arguing and doubting, which are as common as the air we breathe. Be honest. Which do you find easier? Gratitude or grumbling?

We cannot even get close to the presence of God without thanksgiving. The very gates to the glory and power of God are barred from those who would come in with a negative complaining attitude. Faith pleases God because it sees Him for who He is and believes Him for the miraculous. But it also thanks Him for the simplest of things and believes in the hard times that they work together for good.

What is the automatic response when someone compliments us, buys us an unexpected gift or pays a bill for us? We are deeply appreciative. We go out of our way to express to the giver how grateful we are for what they have done for us.

With God, sadly, not so much. We want the "supercalifragilisticexpialidocious" all of the time and when He works slower than we want Him to, we forget who got us up in the morning, who causes our heart to keep beating, who puts food on our table and clothes on our back, who looks after our children, who gives us a great church to attend, who saved us when we were enemies and who laid down His life when we couldn't care less. While we sinned our lives away, He moved heaven and earth to come and die so that we might have life and we grumble and complain because we don't get what we want when we want it.

Perspective, it is all about perspective. Half of what we crave so desperately on our death bed will be meaningless to us unless it is focused on His Kingdom. And if it happens to be a truly selfless, God-centered dream or desire that is on delay, trust Him and praise Him for He is the Alpha and the Omega of the plan and the purpose. It all starts and finishes with Him.

*Daddy, what a glorious God and King You are. I am so grateful to be a part of Your family. I thank You for today, for breath, for sight, for hearing and taste, for love, for grace, for mercy, for friends, flowers, birds, trees and whales and oh how the list can go on.*

## Day 58

### Spirit of Gratitude

**"Rooted and built up in Him and established in the faith, just as you were taught, overflowing with gratitude."** Colossians 2:7

We are continuing where we left off yesterday because of the sheer magnitude of the topic we are looking into. Our human nature, which has been stained by sin, leads us in such a way that we think our reasoning is sound and good and profitable. In the end, however, it proves to be ludicrous and utterly foolish. The age old statement that "the grass is always greener on the other side" has such merit when it comes to why we do some of the things that we do. We have believed a lie from the very start:

- If I had only married Kathy/Tom than my life would be so much better and fulfilled.
- This job cannot be of God. It is a dead end with no hope of any future whatsoever.
- They do not have my best interest at heart; they are in this for themselves.
- If something doesn't change fast, I will never be fulfilled
- How can God say that He loves me when He allowed this evil into my life?

Have you ever felt something like this? We start off blaming life or others or self but then we pull God into the picture and we do the worst thing we could do. We blame the only One who is perfect in all His ways toward us and who can only do what is ultimately the very best thing for us. And besides all that, He can take the worst possible events in our lives, meant to destroy us, and turn them into a testimony of His power and glory.

Divorces, changing careers, accusations, fear, worry and anxiety are all commonplace in the hearts of people everywhere around the world. Hopelessness has taken the place of hopefulness and we are suffering because of it. Gratitude and thanksgiving uproot these lies from the very start and enable us to rest in the love of God, knowing that all things work together for our good if we love God and know that we are called for a holy purpose (Romans 8:28).

- ✓ God choose my spouse and we understand marriage is to make us holy. Happiness is a by-product of Christlikeness, not of being married. Thank You for my spouse.
- ✓ God provided this job and promotion comes from God. No matter how the economy is doing, God is bigger. He provided meat in times of famine to His servant. Thank You for my job.
- ✓ I am called to love everybody—friends, family and enemies. I am not called to compare or to judge, but to love. Like David of old, I will not touch others who report to God. I thank You for the opportunity to love others like You love me.
- ✓ I am content in who I am in Christ. I live to extend Your kingdom in the earth. My fulfillment comes from completing the work You give me to do. Thank You for joy unspeakable and full of glory in me through You.
- ✓ God, You never author evil and so, for this tragedy that I am in, You are preparing to show Your glory through it all. I praise You in advance for the great power You are going to release and the lives that will be touched as You turn this into a testimony for Your name.

*Yes Lord, Yes Lord, I thank you for grace to overcome, grace to win, grace to be all that you want me to be in You.*

## Day 59

## Worship

**"A time will come, however, indeed it is already here, when the true (genuine) worshipers will worship the Father in spirit and in truth (reality); for the Father is seeking just such people as these as His worshipers."** John 4:23 (Amplified)

Man is a worshipper. We were made to worship. The question has never been whether or not we will worship; the question is who we will worship. Will we worship our Creator, our Savior, the Lover of our soul, or will we worship self, money, ideologies, religion, rock stars, athletes, achievement, false gods, fame, etc.? We become what we worship and so our lives will begin to emulate what, for us, is worthy of praise.

Worship is not just what we do at the start of a service; it is how we incorporate into our lives the fullness of who God is. It is how we live for Him. Forgiving those who offend us is an act of worship. Serving our family is an act of worship. Sharing our faith is an act of worship. Living in obedience to the Word of God is an act of worship. Worship encompasses our whole lives, not just moments we set aside to purposefully worship God. The Bible teaches that when the world sees us living in obedience to God and doing God's works – the works that God would do – they will glorify God on our behalf. The more we live out the gospel, the more our lives are worship and will draw those who do not know God into desiring a relationship with Him.

Worship is one of the most central themes in scripture. From the beginning of Genesis, man learns how to approach God in worship. Zechariah 14:17 says, "No worship then you will receive no rain." Psalm 2:12 tells us to kiss the Son lest He be angry with us and we perish. Ensuring that we honor God for who He is determines the amount of His presence and blessing we will have in our lives.

You cannot worship God with all of your heart, mind and strength and then not obey and serve Him. The more you love him, the more you will worship Him; the more you worship Him, the more you will love Him. It is a cycle of intimate relationship. We love Him because He first loved us. When we love Him in return, He comes and visits us and reveals Himself and we in turn love Him more and the personal revival continues unabated until we stop loving and giving (John 14:21).

*Worthy, Worthy, Worthy are you King of Kings and Lord of Lords, I worship Your holy name, Jesus. I lift up my heart in my hands in praise to You for who You are and for what You have done for me. I praise You, I exalt You, I honor You. I adore You and I declare that You are worthy of all praise and all worship. None compares to You, Oh God. No one in all the universe compares to You. Who is Your equal? You have no equals, oh God. No one comes close in all the universe. You are God and God alone and I love You, Lord. I love You, Lord. I Love You.*

Week Four

1. "The very gates to the glory and power of God are barred from those who would come in with a…………..." – fill in the blank
2. When do you never have to wonder if you are praying the will of God?
3. Take some time right now and ask God who needs prayer? Intercede for them right now.
4. What is the cycle of intimate relationship with God?
5. Memorize Philippians 4:6

**The Believer's Lord**

**Day 60**

**The Lamb of God**

**"The next day John saw Jesus coming toward him and said, "Here is the Lamb of God, who takes away the sin of the world!"** John 1:10

We are taking time to look at our Lord and Saviour up close and personal. We do not want to look from a distance but we want to get as close as we possibly can. I do not want to be satisfied knowing about God. I want to know Him personally. I want to proclaim like those of old, "He is MY JESUS" and not just a lofty idea in literature, as some have come to perceive Him. Because He is alive, our relationship with Him should be the same.

King Jesus came to be a blood sacrifice. It is impossible to miss the allusion to the Passover meal and, therefore, the Passover Lamb in the statement that "Jesus is God's Lamb". Sin can only be atoned for by blood, by the death of a sinless, innocent victim willing to lay down its life for another. It would be great if we actually were deserving of someone dying in our place. It is too easy for us on this side of the cross to take for granted the price that was paid. I did not deserve a replacement; I was not owed a substitute. Jesus should never have endured atrocities of the cross in our place. We deserved far worse than the cross for eternity.

Jesus was sinless, the Prince of life, and therefore death had no authority over Him. The Father was so impressed with His Son's sacrifice that He gave Him a name higher than any other name, a name that everybody who ever existed—angel, human and demon—will declare Him as absolute ruler, boss, Master, Lord and God of everything.

Love nailed Jesus to that cross. Love kept Him on the Cross. Love crucified Him so that we could be made new. We are a new creation, with power over sin and with life emanating from us, which creates life in others like sunshine in the spring.

King Jesus fulfilled one of the greatest prophetic types of all by becoming the sacrificial Lamb of God. He poured out His life and in those final minutes uttered the cry, “Father forgive them because they have no idea what they are doing.” There was no retaliation, no anger, no hate, no bitterness, no remorse, no sorrow and no self-pity. Pure perfect, precious love for you and for me produced the cry of forgiveness for the very people taking His life. He was truly the spotless, pure Lamb of God. Through His blood sacrifice on the cross, our sin is utterly and absolutely eradicated from us.

*Oh God, again I say thank You for dying such a death for a worm such as I. For surely, Lord, my response would not have been as Your response was. King Jesus, how great is Your love toward me that while I was in my sin, hating you and despising you, You came and died for me. Overflow me with this wondrous love. In Your Holy Name I ask it.*

## Day 61

## The Good Shepherd

**"I am the good shepherd. The good shepherd lays down his life for the sheep.... [14] "I am the good shepherd. I know My own sheep, and they know Me." John** 10:11, 14

**"The Lord is My Shepherd "Psalm** 23:1

As society has moved from an agricultural society into a commercialized society, the concept of shepherding has been lost. Many books have been written on the topic of shepherding. They sought new words to try and capture the essence of shepherding and so, to name a few, we now have pastoring, coaching, discipling, mentoring, fathering and overseeing. But the reality of it is that all of these speak to just one facet of shepherding.

Jesus is the ultimate Good Shepherd. He sets the perfect example of how one cares for and loves both the individual and the masses. As both the shepherd of the sheep and the doorway to the sheepfold, no one comes into the sheepfold but by His will and command. The Shepherd's heart is clearly seen for He lays down His life for the sheep.

In other parables in scripture, we see how the Shepherd calls each sheep by name and, as the scripture above declares, the sheep know God by His voice. This is an intimate relationship in which the sheep from the time of their birth (salvation experience) would know the voice of the Shepherd who was there when they were birthed, actually calling them into life. The Shepherd is characterized as One who will do anything in His power to protect and defend the sheep. Therefore, a hireling is signified by his unwillingness to lay down his life for the sheep, but instead flees when the wolf appears.

Jesus, like David before Him, goes to war with the enemy of our souls. David killed the lion and the bear with his bare hands. Jesus did one better. While both hands and feet were immobilized, the very act of dying catapulted Him to pre-eminence over every created thing. With hands and feet both nailed, Jesus defeated death and hell. Satan thought he would have free reign over humanity, slaughtering and sacrificing humanity to his heart's content, but he grossly underestimated his Creator. Victory was bought, paid in full, without a word to the enemy. The death of the Shepherd of our souls guaranteed for us victory forever through the power of His life blood.

**"He protects His flock like a shepherd; He gathers the lambs in His arms and carries them in the fold of His garment. He gently leads those that are nursing."** (Isaiah 40:11)

Psalm 23 highlights the ministry of a shepherd, written by the great Old Testament shepherd David. Each verse highlights how God shepherds our lives and teaches us what He is doing during different seasons of our lives. A good shepherd gives to His sheep: relationship, provision, rest, refreshment, healing, guidance, purpose, protection, discipline, hope, consecration, abundance, blessing and security while proving to be ever faithful. Our Great Shepherd specializes in every one of these areas in our lives.

*King Jesus, make me a shepherd like You, one who loves others and enables them to live their lives to the fullest under my loving care.*

## Day 62

## Jesus Is The Way

**I am the way, the truth and the life, no one comes to the Father, but by Me.**
John 14:6

Not too many of us like exclusive clubs or exclusive people. Usually, when we run into something that does not include us, we have a sense of rejection or of not being good enough. And on the other hand, we immediately assume that those who are included feel the opposite—a sense of belonging and of feeling better than others, of privilege and pride.

Such may not be the case but for many it is how they feel. So, some 2000 years ago, itinerant minister Jesus makes the statement that there is only one way to God. And, furthermore, He is that way (or better yet, truer to the original Greek, He is the road, the mode and the means by which any given person can come into an intimate eternal relationship with God). The way to God in the Old Testament, we understand, was a foreshadowing of the New Testament, which is initiated in and through the cross of Christ. His is the blood of the New Covenant.

**G3598** ὁδός hodos *hod-os'* Apparently a primary word; a *road*; by implication a *progress* (the route, act or distance); figuratively a *mode* or *means:* - journey, (high-) way.11

Hebrews 10:20 gives us a further look into the glory of what God was doing and the power of the statement made by Jesus in John 14:6. **"By the new and living way the He has inaugurated for us, through the curtain (that is , His flesh), let us draw near with a true heart in full assurance of faith, our hearts sprinkled clean from an evil conscience and our bodies washed in pure water."**

The same Greek word is used for the new and living way that God had ordained to enable us to come to the Father. It is through the veil of Jesus flesh, the crucifixion made the way for us to come boldly to God because we have been purified. The answer is clear. ``**There is salvation in on one else, for there is no other name under heaven given to people by which we must be saved``** Acts 4:12 The statement of Jesus, the statements of scripture, and the corroborating evidence of changed lives all confirm that Jesus is the only highway to heaven. Whether we are born Hindu, Muslim, Confucian, Asian, African, European, Australian, South American—no matter who we are or what we call ourselves, when it comes to getting to heaven, there is but one way. Jesus. Not because I say so, but because the Word of God says so and that is the most important reason of all. The death of Christ on the cross was for all people. In all the families of the earth, blessing awaits through Jesus the seed of Abraham.

Daddy, it is difficult to except exclusivity, our human nature hates it. What audacity to say that there is only one way to God and yet to be true to Your word and to the Revelation of who YOU are, it makes sense that a Holy God, who is separate and apart from His creation would give us a perfect, WAY to come to Himself. YOU, YOUSELF are the WAY and I give thanks again for the price YOU have paid in making the WAY available.

11. Thayer and Smith. "Greek Lexicon entry for Hodos". "The NAS New Testament Greek Lexicon". . 1999

## Day 63

### Jesus is the Truth

**"I am the truth"** John 14:6

Yesterday, we looked at the statement, "I am the way", which has fuelled debate after debate after debate. Jesus follows up that statement with the statement "I am the truth". Debates rage in the philosophies of man because truth is supposedly unknowable. We have subjective and objective aspects of truth and we have relative and absolute aspects of truth.

God, on the other hand, does not have philosophies concerning what is true or what is truth, for God declares that truth is not philosophy or a way of thinking but instead truth is a Person. Truth is what God says is truth. Truth is a revelation of the character of the Maker of thought itself.

Jesus' declaration that He is the truth causes all who hear it to judge what we think to be truth in a different light. To believe that Jesus is ultimate truth means we must bring our definition and understanding of truth to Him for the final say as to what truth is or what we should believe to be truth. Jesus continually rebuked his disciples for not believing in the supernatural elements of life that were being displayed before their eyes. Peter walked on water. He got out of a boat in the midst of a storm and did what "truth" would say could never happen. But that "truth" met a higher Truth which is faith in God's Word. Truth said to Peter, "If you would like to join me on the water, come. Walk on water to Me." Peter did, until he allowed himself to be distracted by the truth he had grown up with his whole life. Then he began to sink and cried out to Jesus, who immediately lifted him up but not without a reprimand!

You and I have to come to a place of recognizing that God is God. What He says He can do or we can do, through Him can be done. Natural laws must bend to God who alone is Truth. Much of what we see and think to be truth is in fact a distortion of a lie or a deception of God's truth. God is greater even than the natural laws that He put in place and can and will at His discretion overwrite them for His glory, honour and praise.

God can only be pleased by faith and He would never ask us to believe something that is not absolutely trustworthy. Not just trustworthy but even more truth worthy. We can know that God will back up our expectation and hope and faith in Him because we placed our trust in His unfailing truth. Jesus is God's unfailing truth and we can be ever confident that His promises will come to pass in our lives and in the lives of others. This will lead us ultimately to knowing how much He dearly loves us.

*God, I give you my truth and I take Your truth. Your Word says, "Let God be true and every man a liar." That is true when it comes to walking with You. I choose to believe You, period. I do not put confidence in myself but instead in You. I choose You and Your faithful Word.*

## Day 64

### Jesus is the Life

**"I am the Life"** John 14:6

The Bible describes man as a tripartite being. In other words, we are made up of three parts: a spirit, a soul and a body. We are the highest order of physical beings that God created. Through our bodies, we interact with the physical world around us and are aware of others. Through our soul, described by many as our "mind, will and emotions", we are aware of ourselves. Through our spirit, we are aware of God. God created us with three magnificent realities in one body.

Jesus is the life of our physical being, the life of our soul realm and the life of our spirit existence. With Jesus in our lives, all aspects of life have purpose, meaning and vision. Jesus made each of us a new person when He saved us and began revealing His heart to us. The life we are meant to live is wrapped up in God. In Him we live and move and have our being, a poet once said (Acts 17:28). God is Life, so if we want to know what will bring the greatest fulfillment and satisfaction in life, it only makes sense to see that it comes through our relationship with Him. Jesus tells us that He came that we might have an abundant life and eternal life. This starts when we come into relationship with Him (John 10:10; 17:3). Everything about God is about us having a life of meaning, purpose and blessing.

Jesus lived a life on earth that was pleasing to God His Father. When Jesus was baptized, the Father declared Him well pleasing in His sight. No greater joy awaits us than living to bring gladness to the heart of our heavenly Father. Jesus lived life in such a way that He did that very thing and, because of it, God poured out a peculiar anointing on His Son. It was not just the fullness of the Holy Spirit, but something very unique and vital that every one of us would and should desire for our lives.

Psalm 45:7, repeated again in Hebrews 1:9, tells us that Jesus loved righteousness and hated iniquity/lawlessness. Because of this, His Father "anointed him with the oil of joy and gladness". In layman's terms, Jesus so pleased the Father when He clung to what was righteous and holy and rejected what was evil and sinful, that He was anointed with an infectious joy above anybody and everybody. He truly was the happiest man on the planet. I think that tells us why everybody always wanted to be around Him. He brought a view of life that was so radically different from anything people had seen or heard that they could not get enough of who He was.

That way of life is to be our way of life. When we love what is good and hate what is evil, we are truly representing the life the way it was intended to be lived. Like Jesus, we will have a joy unspeakable and full of glory. That is the life we should wish for our children, our friends and our enemies. It is the way of life that is missing on the planet as we try to find joy and fulfillment in things that are disease to our soul and to our bodies. God's way is the best way. His life is the higher life that we are to participate in. Our character allows us to have the benefits of life in Him.

*Daddy, help me to recognize over and over again that You alone are the source of my life, the way in which I come to the greatest fulfillment possible in this life. I thank You for the life that comes from You and You alone.*

## Day 65

## Jesus Our High Priest

**Now the main point of what is being said is this: We have this kind of high priest, who sat down at the right hand of the throne of the Majesty in the heavens, [2] a minister of the sanctuary and the true tabernacle that was set up by the Lord and not man.** Hebrews 8:1,2

The High Priest functions as a mediator between God and man. Jesus, who is both Priest and Sacrifice, has forever fulfilled the requirements that Holiness demanded (1Timothy 2:5). No one else could be our mediator, our go between, our personal stand in the gap, our advocate. No one else could come close to meeting the imperatives of the Father—total sinless perfection. Jesus alone could meet the prerequisite.

Jesus is perfectly positioned to speak to God on God terms as God and to speak to man on man terms as man, for He is both. This is the glory of the incarnation. Job cried out for a mediator (Job 9:32-35), one who could lay hands on God and one who could lay hands on man and bring them to a court room and allow each to be heard and righteous judgment rendered. God did one better. He while staying fully God, became fully man. Jesus laid aside His glory, and as full man, He was tempted to sin in every possible way and yet He never sinned. Who is better positioned to teach us how to overcome sin than someone who has already done it?

Now consider for a moment that your mediator and High Priest has also been your sacrifice. How intimately committed to your success is He? He did not offer someone else on the altar of sacrifice to appease God's wrath; He offered Himself. As our High Priest, He shows His own blood to the Father for our forgiveness and covering. This should produce in us the utmost confidence and thanksgiving for so great a sacrifice. Our Jesus is absolutely committed to us and has already proven that He will never leave us or forsake us. He had the chance in the garden to leave but choose instead to die in our place.

*King Jesus, how great is Your love for me. How amazing to consider that You are both Priest and Sacrifice. I am overwhelmed at the evidence of Your love for me.*

*Let me never forget or doubt that the greatest of all sacrifices was when you died for me. I come boldly to Your throne because of Your great sacrifice.*

## Day 66

## Jesus The Great Shepherd

**"I am the Good Shepherd"** John 10:1

Read Psalm 23

In Mark 10:18, when someone came and called Jesus good, He somewhat rebuked them by saying, "Only God is good, so don't call me good." And yet, in John 10:1, He declares Himself good. Is it a contradiction or is He Jesus, Good/God Himself? Jesus knew that He was both Good and that He Himself was God. It is the rich young ruler who did not accept the divinity of Christ and he proves it by not heeding the directions that God/Jesus gave to him.

David declared the Lord as his shepherd and that He was the one who would lead and guide him. Jesus declares in the New Testament that He is the embodiment of this Old Testament declaration. It is a call to us that we should embrace His care and direction.

We don't understand shepherding much these days in that we have moved so far away from this way of life. There are numerous key thoughts that could be highlighted in the principle of a shepherd, but the one I would like to draw attention to is that of how a shepherd would lead and guide his sheep into different pastures for feeding. Sheep are notorious for stripping ground bare of its grasses and leaving very little for regrowth. Thus the hatred relationship between cattlemen and shepherds.

There are times in our lives when God is leading us in very different pastures. There is food to eat, but it may not be to our liking. Scriptures tells of events in which angels prepared food for men. Upon eating it was sweet in their mouth but bitter in their stomach (Revelations 10:9-10). When God leads us into desert times or trains us in disappointment, it has more to do with making us like Him than any other thing. Responding how He would respond qualifies us for greater usage. Staying in immaturity and mediocrity simply will not do. God knows the potential of Himself in each of us as we unlock His power to the world around us.

God loves us as we are, but He also loves us to much to allow us to stay that way. If we could see from God's perspective the power that abides in us and the glory that is upon us, we would shake our heads in disgust that we allow ourselves to wallow when God has planned for us to reign. Princes and princesses are made to reign and, as sons and daughters to the King of the universe, it is only right that we think, plan, pray and expect like royalty. The Shepherd of the sheep is preparing us to rule with Him so, when you are in a season that is not that comfortable, not what you expected or somewhat frustrating, look from heaven's perspective where you are seated with Him and realize, "This too shall pass". Victory is ours for the taking as we understand the greatest victory is over ourselves.

*Father, thank You for Your commitment to not leave me as You found me. You are working Your perfect will out in me, transforming me into Your image. To this process I say yes and amen.*

## Month Three

## The Believer's Lord

### Week One

1. What nailed Jesus to the cross and what kept Him on the cross?
2. Explain how Jesus is perfectly positioned to speak to God?
3. God intended that we reign in life but what do too many of us actually end up doing?
4. Pick a verse to memorize this week.

## Day 67

### Resurrection is a Person

**"Jesus said to her, I am the resurrection and the Life, the one who believes in Me, even if he dies, will live. Everyone who lives and believes in Me, will never die - ever. Do you believe this?"** John 11:25, 26

I have to stop for a moment as I ponder these words of the Lord Jesus. When I first was saved, God stirred my heart with love for His Word. I simply could not get enough of it. So shortly after being saved, I began memorizing God's Word, a verse a day for a year. The very first verse I ever memorized is the verse we are looking at today.

Jesus' best friend has died. Jesus has delayed coming to see Lazarus, allowing him to die, for God had a bigger purpose in mind. The grief of Mary and Martha, Lazarus' sisters, was inconsolable. Jesus came into the scene knowing fully why He was there and what He was about to do.

Jesus had already raised many people from the dead at this point of ministry. No one, however, had been dead for more than a day or two. Jewish tradition stated that the spirit did not leave the body till after the third day. So for someone to be raised from the dead after the third day would be truly impossible, for the spirit of the person had left to the judgment of eternal states. Martha and Mary had resolved that it was too late for Lazarus to be raised. They believed Jesus would raise Lazarus on the Day of Judgment at the end of time. But Jesus questioned their faith: Is your faith in your traditions or in the truth of who I am? The resurrection is not a time; it is a person. Destiny does not call people from their graves to answer for their lives. God Himself calls forth all creation to give account. The Resurrection is a person not an event.

Jesus is making it clear that the limitations that they have put on Him must be removed. "I am the resurrection, I raise the dead, I call them forth, and it is based on my personal will and desire, not on a destined time." Jesus had proved this already in His earthly ministry, but now on this day, He calls Lazarus forth. Death was never God's plan. We were made to live forever. Death is a consequence of sin. Heaven is a return to God's original plan. No death, no sickness, and no disease. Consider that every person who has ever lived was never meant to die. In other words, would you like to have a conversation with Abraham, Moses, Martin Luther, Smith Wigglesworth, Abraham Lincoln or a loved one who has passed away? In God's order they would have never died in the first place.

God, in resurrecting the dead, shows us His plan and purpose. He hates death and separation. He gives a foretaste of what heaven will be like, a foretaste of eternity. He conquered it before and, once and for all, it will have no more power. Should we be surprised that God commands us in Christ to raise the dead? The disciples did it and down through history we see other servants of God fulfilling the mandate of the Word by raising the dead. If we would be honest we see it as an impossible feat. We must see death from God's, His hatred of death and sin and Satan's use of it to keep people in fear. When we see death and sickness from God's perspective that will be the time in which the world of the supernatural will open to us in greater measure.

*Miraculous God, there is no one like You. How awesome You are and how moved by Your love for Your creation. It is so clear that You only desire what is the absolute best for us. Help us to know Your love. It answers all our questions. Fill me up and let me overflow with love for others.*

## Day 68

## The Servant

**So He got up from supper, laid aside His robe, took a towel, and tied it around Himself. [5] Next, He poured water into a basin and began to wash His disciples' feet and to dry them with the towel tied around Him.** John13:4.5

Jesus is preparing to leave the disciples. It is just before their last meal together and Jesus knows He is going to be betrayed and crucified. One thing is left for Him to do. Although He has spent His earthly life modeling His heart and mind to His disciples and although He has taught them this lesson over and over again, the last night is the perfect night for Him to show them in action what He has been modeling for three and a half years.

If you have lost a loved one, your last minutes with them are forever etched in your being. You cannot forget those precious moments. Though Jesus would be raised and truly alive, still these last moments with His disciples would echo in their significance throughout the church age. Jesus dismisses the servants, He puts on a towel and He kneels down and begins to wash His disciples' feet.

Living in a day and an age where slavery and servants are no longer commonplace, it is hard for us to fully grasp this event. I can remember going to Uganda for the first time in my life and, shortly after being there, having young girls and older women kneel as they greeted me. My immediate reaction was to pull them up and not allow this to happen to me or to them. Though I spiritualized it, for kneeling is an act of worship, for them it was more similar to the act of bowing that is common in the Japanese culture. It is a show of respect and honor as well as a greeting. My friends explained this time and again to me, but I never got used to it.

In Israel, slaves, indentured servants and women did the menial tasks of the day. Men and those in authority were served and did not serve. No doubt, as in any culture, it would then become the desire of most men to be in the highest offices so they could receive such treatment. Jesus, in taking the towel and basin and washing the feet of His disciples, blows their minds. So unbecoming is this to Peter that He refuses to be washed by Jesus. Jesus' answer is stunning.

Can we stop for a moment here? God is washing the feet of man, our stinky, dirty, poopy feet. Is this for real? Am I actually beginning to see the picture? The God of heaven is washing my feet. I don't know that I can fully fathom that. Me falling like a dead man before Him, I can fathom. Me, weeping for my sins at His feet, I can fathom. Me, crying out for mercy and grace to minister His love to others, I can fathom. But Jesus washing our feet, God loving us so much that He literally serves our needs, is at times a stretch for us to fully comprehend. And yet He does it every minute of every day. The air we breathe, the food we eat, the clothes we wear, the jobs we work, the homes we live in are all the product of a loving Father who meets our needs in love and gentle care.

Jesus words set the stage: "If I, your Lord and Master, serve you, I don't think you should have a problem serving one another." Do we have a problem serving one another? Is it not because we do not know who we are in Him? King Jesus, God of the universe, washing our feet, dying for our sins and we have issues serving one another! We serve Jesus and we look like Jesus when we serve others. He is greatly honored and pleased when we follow in His example.

*Show me the feet, Lord, and I will do the rest.*

## Day 69

### Betrayed and the Rejected For Me

**He was despised and rejected by men, a man of suffering who knew what sickness was. He was like someone people turned away from; He was despised, and we didn't value Him**. Isaiah 53:3

Have you ever felt betrayed or rejected? Maybe for some of you it was not a feeling at all but was in fact a reality. Humanity is famous for our mistreatment of one another. The very first brothers on the planet ended up in a murder, a brutal murder that came about because of jealousy and envy (Genesis 4:1-8). So if we see such horrendous results in the very first family, it is little wonder that rejection and betrayal are commonplace.

The human heart was not meant for rejection, but for love and acceptance. The greatest need in mankind is to be loved and accepted. We will go to great, great lengths to be accepted and have a sense of belonging.

The Bible says that Jesus, the Son of God, came to His own people, King of the Jews, Saviour of the nation, but was instead rejected and turned aside. The Gentiles were more ready than the Jews to receive the Messiah foretold for thousands of years. The words of Nicodemus echo in my ears, "We (the Pharisees) know that you have been sent by God, for no one can do the miracles you do unless God is with Him" (John 3). The parables of Jesus tell us that the Sanhedrin rejected and crucified Him out of jealousy, not because they did not know who He was.

But the rejection by Israel, the betrayal by Judas, His disciples running from Him when He needed them the most and the cry on the cross, "My God, My God, why have you forsaken me" tells us that Jesus' heart must have endured what no other heart could ever endure.

In my youthful understanding of these events I use to proudly declare, "He was rejected, so that I might always be accepted." It is true and has great merit, but it does not mean that you will not experience times and seasons where you endure rejection for your faith, rejection by friends and family and even rejection by churches that you love and are trying to bless. It does not mean that a blanket of acceptance is placed over you and you can only experience bountiful relationships. T.D. Jakes once said (and I paraphrase), "If Christ felt rejected of His own Father, what makes you think you won't go through times and seasons of feeling the same?" Prepare for that season now by knowing in your spirit that feelings lie but the Word of God is eternally true. God can never forsake or reject you in Christ. You have been bought and paid for with the precious blood of the Lamb.

Jesus' rejection may be a foreshadowing of seasons we may have to endure, but there is a difference. He has promised never to forsake us and never to leave us alone. Now that is the truth. On that we can stand. Because of Christ's death on the cross for us, we are beloved and will never be forsaken of God.

You are with me. That is all I need to know. I can go through anything as long as You are with me.

## Day 70

## The Father Revealed

**"To see me is to see the Father."** John 14:9 The Message

**"Who being the brightness of *His* glory and the express image of His person,"** Hebrews 1:3

**"For the entire fullness of God's nature dwells bodily in Christ,"** Colossians2:9

John 13-17 are Jesus' last hours with His disciples before He is to be crucified. These moments are of great significance. If you have a red letter edition Bible, the pages are filled with red as Jesus speaks His heart and thoughts to His disciples. There are key messages He wants to give to them and takes this time alone with them to teach them. One comment in particular that Jesus makes is, "To see me is to see the Father" (John 14:9)

When you see Jesus in your mind's eye or in your heart, do you see the Father? In Jesus' earthly ministry, He makes it crystal clear that He did nothing that was not divinely orchestrated from above. He spoke what the Father Spoke. He did what the Father would do. He healed who the Father wanted healed. So why, after 2000 years of Christian history, do we still have such a wrong view of God the Father? I don't think that we can put the whole blame on our earthly father's failures. As the church of Jesus Christ, are we clearly revealing that Jesus is the truest expression and the actual exact representation of who God is and what God does?

- When a woman is caught in adultery instead of authorizing her death, Jesus not only forgives her, He confirms she is not condemned. (John 8:1-11)
- Jesus visits a traitorous thief who immediately repents (Luke 19:1-9)
- When a Wedding runs out of wine Jesus steps in and provides phenomenal wine. (John 2:1-11)
- Jesus personally goes to Jarius's house to raise her from the dead. (Luke 8:40-56)
- Jesus works on the Sabbath day by healing a paralytic (Matthew 13:9 - 14)

I could keep going but I think we have enough here to process. Now, replace "Jesus" with "the Father" in each sentence. The heartbeat of Jesus was and is the heartbeat of the Father. We must remind ourselves it was the Father who sent His only beloved Son into the world so that we might have access back into the Father's love for us. We have a religious, judgmental, cynical, harsh view of God the Father that must go the way of the dinosaur. It must die the death and be resurrected to the true Biblical picture of a loving Father who runs to meet His wayward child for whom He has been daily looking and pacing, waiting for their return.

The Father reaches down to the adulteress and cleanses her, puts new clothes on her, cleanses her from shame, hugs her in His love, beautifies her from within and gives her a family. The Father takes the rejected, hated tax collector, the betrayer of his people, and calls him out and says, "To your house I want to come, even though everybody else has rejected you. I know you by name and I want to spend time with you." The Sabbath became greater than God ever intended it to, where the Sabbath was more important than man. The Sabbath was for man's benefit. Father God, turned the tables and set it straight. It is always right to do good, no matter the day.

*Daddy, my cry is to know You for who You truly are. Take all vestiges of religious ideas of You from my heart and let the truth of You be revealed to me. I want to know You for who You are so that I might draw the world to You.*

## Day 71

## Jesus, the Son of God

**Read John 3:16/ John 19:7**

In the Bible, the Gospel writers tell the life story of Jesus from different perspectives. Each one of them tells the story highlighting different aspects of it for the specific audience to which they are ministering. For example, John does not go into the details of Jesus before Caiaphas and Annas, the leaders of the Sanhedrin. But it is there that Jesus clearly annunciates before them that He is the Son of God and it is upon this statement that the High Priest finalizes the fate of Jesus in his mind. Jesus clearly communicates in His speech, through His miracles, how He prayed, His intercession on the cross and in His resurrection that He is the Son of God. As Jesus declared to Nicodemus in John 3, "For God so loved the world that He sent His only beloved Son into the world." Jesus is that Son, unlike Isaac whose life was spared and was lifted up off of the altar to be replaced by a ram (Genesis 22). Jesus was the Lamb of God who freely offered up Himself for us so that the penalty of sin might be removed from our lives.

What has always made Christianity a difficult faith to understand is the teaching of the Trinity—that God is Father, Son and Holy Spirit, three distinct persons, but one Triune God. In eternity past, before Creation, God the Father, knowing that man would sin and corrupt themselves, turned to God the Son and sought to know whether He would willingly go and lay down His life as the incarnate Son of God (1 Peter 1:19-20).

We see the Triune God working in creation as He declares, "Let us make man in our image" (Genesis1:27-28). We see the Triune God in Christ's baptism when He declares, "This is My beloved Son" and the Spirit is poured out over the Son (Matthew 3:17). We hear Jesus in His last discourse with His disciples speak so clearly of the Spirit's divinity and we are made aware of how heinous it is to blaspheme the Holy Spirit. (John 16:5-16)

Scripture is filled with symbols, types and names that speak to the personality and identity of each of the Godhead, but though they can be individually identified, they cannot be separated from each other as three Gods. No, that would be heresy and false doctrine. The Word of God shows us that there is but one God, but three distinct, divine Persons that comprise God.

For the Jewish mindset, to declare oneself the Son of God, was to declare oneself God. The only equivalent for us today would be to for you and me to begin tell everybody we meet that we are God Almighty in the flesh.

No Jewish person would dare make such a blasphemous claim, on pain of death. For Jesus to make such a claim, knowing the outcome, is simply another testimony of its validity. Truth cannot lie and Jesus could no more deny His divinity than we can deny our humanity. The testimony in accepting His Sonship is to accept the Father's great, great, great love for us. For if the Father sent His only beloved Son to die for us, what value has He just placed on each of us? That you and I in our wretched sin-filled status should have the perfect, righteous, holy, sinless Son of God die in our place.

Martin Luther once declared, "Oh for a Thousand Tongues to sing, my great redeemers praise." Take some time right now and meditate and worship God for His plan of salvation so great and awesome. Jesus took the pain and rejection that we might know the Joy and acceptance that only God can give would be ours both now in time and for eternity to come.

## Day 72

## I AM

God replied to Moses, "I AM WHO I AM" This is what you are to say to the Israelites: I AM has sent me to you." Exodus 3:14

There are times in our lives when we are apprehended by God. No way around it. God, who always has the upper hand, backs us into a corner and asks of us something that we may not be so inclined to give. In Exodus 3, Moses was in such a situation. He was 80 years old and at rest in himself. His dreams of being a savior of sorts were well removed from his psyche. He had married, had children and settled down.

One day, God showed up and said, "You are the man." Moses was not so sure. He would've rather seen someone else take on the task. God persisted, however, almost to the point of anger. Moses considered the options and asked God, "When they ask me the name of the God of Abraham, Isaac and Jacob, what shall I answer?" God answered with the now famous, "I AM THAT I AM." Matthew Henry explains, "*I am that I am.* Being self-existent, He cannot but be self-sufficient, and therefore all-sufficient, and the inexhaustible fountain of being and bliss."15

Moses was satisfied with this and reverentially taught God's people the reality of the revelation. God is, God was and God will always be. He needs nothing and He is our everything. Everything that we need, we can and will find in Him. The glorious reality of this is that the history of the nation of Israel is founded on name after name being linked to this revelation of God. I Am That I Am – is what we pronounce as Jehovah or for Hebrews Yahweh. But Jehovah becomes linked to further fulfillments of this very truth.

- Jehovah Shalom – the Lord our Peace (Judges 6:24)
- Jehovah Tsedeq – The Lord our Righteousness (Jeremiah 23:6)
- Jehovah Jireh – The Lord will Provide (Genesis 22:14)
- Jehovah Rapha – The Lord our Healer (Exodus 15:26)
- Jehovah Nissi – The Lord our Banner (Exodus 17:15)

As God continues to reveal the fullness of His character and glory to His people, the people of God connect the revelation to His name. It is forever a testimony of who God is and what He will do in our lives as we put our trust in Him and live in obedience to His ways. Have you ever needed peace, righteousness, provision, healing or a standard to follow? Well, we find this and so much more in God. His names reveal who He is and who He desires to be in us.

Jesus' ministry on earth proved His willingness to heal and deliver. Yet, when He went to His own home town, they did not receive Him as the Messiah and so He could do only a few miracles there. He desired to heal, revive, deliver as is His name, but their mindset against Him limited them from the glory of God made available to them (Matthew 13:54-58).

Beware, for you and I can do the same. Our doubts and fears put God in a box that He simply cannot fit in, but that is the size and shape of the God we construct and we miss out on the fullness of who He Is and what He desires to do.

Daddy, I take You out of my self-imposed box. I want all of who You truly are, no chains and no limitations based on my fears or others misunderstandings. I want to know You.

15. esword, Matthew Henry Complete Commentary, Published in 1708-1714, public domain, Comments on Exodus 3:14

## Day 73

### Jesus the "I AM"

**57The Jews replied, "You aren't 50 years old yet, and You've seen Abraham?"[58] Jesus said to them, "I assure you: Before Abraham was, I am."[59] At that, they picked up stones to throw at Him. But Jesus was hidden and went out of the temple complex** John 8:57-59

King Jesus is the Great I Am. If no other testimony about these things came from the pages of the gospel; it would be clear without a shadow of a doubt who King Jesus thought of himself. Jesus declared Himself to be God in the flesh. That would constitute blasphemy, unless it was true. The Jews fully understood the implication He was making. The fact that immediately their judgment was stoning tells you how much they understood what He was trying to communicate!

This ultimately became the charge that cost Him his life for you and for me. Though we know they delivered Him to Pilate because of jealousy and envy, the charge against him was blasphemy and proclaiming himself a king. On both counts He was innocent and should not have been condemned. Instead He went to the cross and laid down His life for us, fulfilling scripture after scripture. Jesus is the Lamb of God; He is the suffering Servant; He is the snake lifted up in the wilderness; and He is our Propitiation. All these names, titles and symbols are fulfilled in Him. Jesus is the great I AM. He is our peace. He is our righteousness. He is our Provision. He is our Healing. The challenge now is for us to tap into the reservoir of God's unlimited supply, even as God did for Israel in rescuing them from captivity; Jesus has done so much more defeating Satan and making a full display of Satan's defeat at the cross.

Jesus' entire ministry was under the Old Covenant primarily instituted at Sinai and Horeb in the Dessert. Now that Jesus has gone through the cross and is seated at the right hand of the Father, the veil has been rent and we participate in the greatest of all covenants. All of His promises are yes and amen. The greatest failure on our part is that we do not ask God with the understanding that we are not paupers but heirs, royalty. In this place of royalty and in this place of being heirs, we are authorized to expect a particular response from God according to His will. All of this is only made possible because of who God is as the Great I Am. When we see God for who He truly is, we can believe and expect the miraculous in our lives.

Imagine with me for a moment that you are an heir to a fortune and it has been hidden from you your whole life. One day, you are found to be the heir and the entire fortune is at your disposal. Oh the work that you could accomplish with the fortune! It would not just meet your immediate needs and those of your family, but it would impact the world around you for good. But instead you choose to stay the way you are. You made it this far without all the extras and the possibilities. You make up your mind that it would just be too great of a change and too much of a responsibility to take on the role of being a billionaire and you know you simply don't have the training to handle the roles forced on you.

That would seem insane to most of us, but the reality is that is how most of us treat the authority and power invested in us by the New Covenant. We do not war for healing, for deliverance, for salvation or for turning the world upside down. But that is God's business and that is the high and holy call that He has placed on every believer—to know Him for who He truly is and to change the world back to its glorious condition.

*Daddy, keep opening my eyes. Keep helping me to dream and to have vision for holy interactions in my life on a daily basis. Let a holy fire and a holy boldness rise up in my heart to challenge the norms and to create change in lives around me. I anticipate Your power and Your glory being revealed through me.*

## Day 74

### Commander of the Lord's Army

**He replied. "I have now come as Commander of the LORD's army**." Joshua 5:13-15

Moses has died. Joshua has become his successor and God has spoken to Joshua and told him to be strong and courageous. Joshua had been Moses' servant and, even after Moses would leave the tabernacle, Joshua would stay on in God's presence (Exodus 33:11). Now he has brought the nation of Israel to the doorstep of battle. They have not yet engaged the enemy but they have experienced God with them similar to what they had experienced with Moses. But a change is about to take place. Where God fought for them before and they could stand and see the salvation of the Lord, now they too must enter into the battle and see how God will fight with them and through them.

God chose to give Joshua a personal revelation of Himself quite different than what Moses had ever received. Moses first knew the voice of God through a fiery bush that needed no fuel in which to burn. Neither the flame nor the bush diminished. God revealed Himself to Moses as the Great I AM, the all-sufficient one, needing nothing but providing everything.

To Joshua, however, God revealed Himself as a Man with a sword drawn in His hand. Joshua wanted to know, "Are you for us or against us?" The answer was, "Neither. I am Captain of God's Armies both heavenly and earthly." Joshua bowed in worship: "What does my Lord want to say to His servant?" The details of the conversation are withheld from us, with the exception of one. This is the only other time in scripture that one is commanded to remove their sandals for the ground they are upon is now holy. It was holy because Joshua was in the presence of God Himself—not an angel, but a physical manifestation of the living God. Theology calls this a *Theophany*, an Old Testament revelation of Jesus.

Joshua of the Old Testament meets Joshua of the New Testament (what we call Jesus, they call Yeshua or Joshua) and the immediate response is one of worship. The one and only Saviour, the true leader of God's armies, is our King of Kings and Lord of Lords the Lord Jesus Christ. Joshua is standing on holy ground because of the presence of the true leader of the armies of God. The enemies of our God do not stand a chance. Joshua sees the true commander and chief.

It must have been a life changing moment. Here I am Joshua. See for yourself. I am a Mighty God of War. I will oversee and help you through. You are not in this alone. Like David after him, Joshua was a great military strategist because he followed God's lead. There is a prophetic prototype here for us to follow. Joshua brought God's people into the Promised Land; Jesus will bring God's people into our Promised Land.

This is not just the heavenly land, which we should all wonderfully anticipate, but the Promised Land for us today embodies in the promises of God in scripture, revealed to us by His Spirit for our specific lives. Whatever the promise, Jesus has already made it available and is the assurance that you will receive it. We, like Joshua of old, must follow His lead; obey each command; fight in faith; never, never, never give up; and walk into the fulfillment of each promise God has for us.

Daddy, I press into Your promises for me. I press into achieving all that You have for me. I stake my claim to the blessings and provision of God paid for by King Jesus. I do not take lightly the price that He paid so that I could live in Your promises. I gratefully receive them and encourage others to walk in them as well.

## Week Two

1. God intended that we use our ruling nature with .........? And our serving nature with ........?
2. Jesus set the example of serving by washing the feet of the disciples, is there a person or persons that you can purposefully go out of your way and serve? In prayer ask God to show you who you can purpose to serve this week.
3. Are you comfortable seeing Jesus as the exact representation of God the Father? Is it easy for you to replace the deeds of Jesus with the deeds of God the Father?
4. Do you see that you are a Spiritual Billionaire? Have you made up your mind that you will unlock the treasuries of heaven or is it just easier to live the status quo Christian life?
5. Quote last week's memory verse and pick a new verse for this week.

## Day 75

### Christ our Intercessor

**As You sent Me into the world, I also have sent them into the world.** John 17:18

The night before Jesus laid down His life on our behalf, He took time alone with His Father. If there is one thing we must first look at when considering the prayer of Christ, it is that fifteen verses are spent praying for the very first believers, seven verses are spent praying for those who would come to faith by their testimony and five verses are spent praying for Himself. The point simply is seen in His selflessness and love for others. King Jesus is going to die. He is about to lay His life down for us, but instead of praying for Himself, the majority of His time is praying for present and future believers.

Prayer is a place of honesty and intimacy. You cannot pretend to be something you are not. In prayer, who you truly are and what you truly feel is going to influence how you pray. King Jesus taught us that out of the abundance of the heart the mouth speaks. Though we apply this mainly to our regular conversations, it is true of our conversations with God. What tends to amaze people when they read the book of Psalms is the honesty of the writers. They wear their emotions on their sleeve. You know in an instant if the writer is having a good day or a bad one. They did not mince words with God and God does not desire that we try to sound a certain way when we pray. The reality is if we are going to move God at all, it will only be because we are honest and from the heart.

King Jesus is expressing His deepest heart; it is one of the last prayers He will pray on earth. Among the numerous phrases I would love to highlight from this prayer, Jesus tells us that as He has been sent, so we have been sent. He had a supernatural birth, and we have had a supernatural birth, (John1:12-13; 3:7). He had a majestic baptism and we have had a majestic baptism (I Corinthians 12:13). He had a Spirit Baptism and we should have had a Spirit Baptism (Acts 1:8). So we can see clearly from scripture that God looks down and says to each and every one of us, "Your foundation is fantastic; your starting place is awesome." God has made all the provision for success that we need.

Jesus changed the world around Him and was willing to lay down His life out of love. So how are we doing with that? That would be the challenge for the Church of Jesus Christ. We know the vision and the plan and the purpose, but do we know our power and our enablement by the Spirit to complete the task? The promise of God is that the prayer of Jesus will be answered and it will be in this last day that the power of God will enable the people of God to fulfill the will of God in this generation.

Father, thank You for my supernatural birth, for my glorious baptism and for my divine enablement through the Baptism of the Holy Spirit. I choose to be an instrument in Your hand to reveal Your love to the world around me, just like Jesus.

## Day 76

### The Resurrected Christ

**" Don't cling to me," Jesus told her "for I have not yet ascended to the Father, go to my brothers and tell them that I am ascending to My Father and your Father - to My God and your God"** John 20: 17

Jesus is the resurrected Christ. He told us before He left that there would be many who would come in His name and declare that they were the anointed, chosen of God and could give you the true meaning of life. Please note, for all who have said that they were God's chosen salvation for mankind, their tombs are full. King Jesus, His tomb is empty. His resurrection was God the Father's seal of approval that He and He alone fulfilled the laws demand. His blood and His blood alone frees us from sin. His name and His name alone saves us and grants us access to the throne room of heaven.

The order in which Jesus made His statement to Mary in John 20:17 is worth consideration. Jesus said He was ascending to "My Father and your Father" before He said, "My God and your God". To this day, we still struggle to see and know God as our Father the way that Jesus revealed the Father to us. Numerous scholars have commented on how Jesus opened the eyes of the Jews of His day and of the believer to the understanding and the intimate relationship God desires to have with us as His dearly beloved –not as paupers, rejects, rebels, prodigals and the wayward, but as sons and daughters, princes and princesses, co-regents, priests and overcomers. Here is our Lord and Master declaring to us, "Let me go. Don't hold me down. I am going to the Father. Tell my brothers. I am ascending to Daddy and Sovereign."

Matthew Henry Commentary and Jamison, Faussett and Brown Commentary both comment that this is the first time that Jesus uses the word "brothers"14. We are known throughout His earthly ministry as disciples, followers, servants and friends, but now, after their betrayal, their cowardice and their fear, He lovingly forgives and declares, "Tell my brothers, I am going to Abba." Through Christ and in Christ, we come to know God as Abba, for that is who the Father is to the Son. The language that Jesus used in His earthly life was Aramaic and both in Aramaic and in Hebrew it is the word used for Father.  In His humanity Christ reveals to us the True and living God and so in Him as well we recognize that our

Abba is also God Almighty, terrible in power, awesome in splendor, fearful in glory, to be lovingly known but honorably feared and worshipped.

To know God as Abba is the relationship that God Himself longs for us to live in. The picture of heaven is without a doubt an ongoing, ever deepening revelation of the love affair between God and us. Children of the Father and the Bride of Christ are relational terms used to help us know the greatness of His love for us. We were never meant to cling to our natural, finite revelation of who God is. We must have a supernatural, infinite, illuminating revelation of God as our Father.

God, it is not my desire to just know You in my mind and through sound theological doctrine. Abraham, Moses, David, Isaiah, Daniel and, in particular, the disciples experienced You in profound and supernatural ways. It is my desire to know You in those same supernatural dimensions. Let the eyes of my heart be opened to see and to know, to understand and to experience Your great love toward us.

14. Henry, Matthew. "Complete Commentary on John 20:1". "Matthew Henry Complete Commentary

## Day 77

## The Word of God

**"In the beginning was the Word, and the Word was with God, and the Word was God."** John 1:10

I have worked in a bookstore for a number of years. Solomon, some three thousand years ago, said that there is never an end to books being written. Every book written in all the languages of the world, every sentence, every word used has meaning and purpose because it identifies with the intent of the user. One of the titles of Jesus is that He is "the Word".

Most obviously, there is no word like this Word. He is the embodiment of the speaker, who happens to be God the Father. What He spoke has put on flesh. The Word was with God and the Word was God. Jesus then is the personification of God's words. He is not like man who speaks lies, makes promises and breaks them, signs contracts and fails to fulfill the requirements. God is Holy. He is sinless and perfect and, therefore, every promise He has ever made will be fulfilled. All that is in the character of God, that caused Him to speak to man—the covenants, the revelations, the illuminations, the wisdom, the purposes of God, put on flesh and we call Him Jesus. When we doubt the "Word" of God, we doubt the veracity of Jesus. When we choose to reject the principles of the Word, we reject the person and character of God Himself.

Of all the speeches known to man, one is stilled hailed as the greatest spoken of all times. They come from this "Word". We call this speech the Sermon on the Mount. King Jesus lays out for His disciples how we should live if we want to be like Him (Matthew 5-7). No atheist or agnostic can read these words and deny their impact. The love and the grace and the wisdom are self-evident in what is spoken. Jesus' ministry was filled with gracious, powerful, life-changing utterances.

You have been reading the scriptures for some days now. The disciples had been with Jesus for three and half years hearing His message and learning of His ways. But after the resurrection and their salvation experience, the risen Christ in Luke 24:45 opened their minds that they might understand the scriptures. We have heard many people argue about how, amidst the many denominations of Christianity, there are different interpretations of the scriptures. The scriptures make it clear, however, that there is to be one faith. The scriptures are not open to private interpretation but are God-breathed. (2 Timothy 3:16) God, being the author of the Word must also be the illuminator, revealer and instructor of His Word. If the disciples needed a move of the Holy Spirit on their minds to properly discern the Word, then we surely need the same.

*Take a minute right now and ask God to do the same for you.*

## Day 78

## The Word of God

**The Word became flesh and took up residence among us.** John 1:14

As He stood before His accusers before His death, the Word was silent for my sake (Matt.26:63; 27:14; Mark 15:4-5). The Voice that called creation into existence paused. The Word that created the universe with His voice chose to be speechless. The Voice that is so necessary to life itself was silenced.

The scriptures we hold in our hands the "God-breathed" record that God desired that we should have, should be precious to each and every one of us. Take the time to study history and you will see not only the murders of prophets and apostles, but also of translators for working so hard to get the written testimony of the living Word into our hands. Satan has fought its transmission through the centuries and, too sadly, we disregard the written aspect and the "Person" aspect of the Word. You cannot love Jesus and despise the Word of God; nor can you love the written Word and not love the true Word to whom it points.

We must consider for a moment that God has not stopped incarnating Himself. His perfect plan has been that His glory would fill everything that He created (we will save this topic for further study). Jesus is the express image of that glory and, according to His High Priestly prayer in John 19, that glory has been shared with you and with me. We are to reveal it to the world around us.

Whether it is through asking forgiveness, giving forgiveness, sharing our faith, acts of mercy or the good works of the Holy Spirit expressed through signs and wonders, God's resources are endless. Will we be like the little boy who gives what is in our hand to Jesus for Him to do with as He pleases (John 6:9)? Will we be like Moses and lay down the rod of our occupation and significance and allow God to have all of us? (Exodus 4:1-5) When we do, He does wonders beyond our wildest dreams.

*Daddy God, thank You for preserving Your words down through the centuries, enabling the scriptures to be passed down generation after generation. Thank You for ensuring that I would have a copy of Your truth to learn more about who*

*You are. Let those working in translation be ever so blessed and quickened, enabling people groups who do not have Your Word to be blessed and know the Word.*

*Daddy, we pray for a fuller understanding of Your Word. Let the Word of God dwell in our hearts and minds richly. We pray for holy transformation of how we live and think so that we can be the expression of who You are to a lost and dying world. God, we pray for the leaders You have ordained to teach and preach Your Person. Give them fresh illumination, fresh revelation, that they would bring hot bread and hot meat to the table so that your people woul (Exodus 3:d be filled with You and desire with all that is within them to give what they have away. Let us be like Peter and John and, in the marketplace of life, say, "Worldly riches I do not have, but what I have I give to you. In the name of Jesus of Nazareth rise and be healed."*

## Day 79

## Another Comforter Just Like Me

**Nevertheless, I am telling you the truth. It is for your benefit that I go away, because if I don't go away the Counselor will not come to you. If I go, I will send Him to you.** John 16:7

Today, we will look in-depth at the Holy Spirit. John 16 is one of the great scriptures that reveal the Spirit. The Greek word for "another" infers fully that the Holy Spirit is a Comforter, Helper and Counsellor "just like Jesus".

Jesus is the prototype for which the Holy Spirit works. Jesus is our Comforter. Jesus is our Helper. Jesus is our first Counsellor. The Holy Spirit takes who Jesus is and minsters Him to us. The way Jesus personally cared for each person to whom He ministered while on earth is a picture for us to know that He desires to do the same for us. This means that the precious Holy Spirit will come to you in a profound and powerful way, for He dwells within you.

Jesus was excited at the Holy Spirit's coming for He knew that, within our spirits, God Himself would take up residence. Without the cross and Jesus' departure, that simply could not happen. Now, however, every believer everywhere is a virtual ark of the covenant, a safe with the greatest treasure known to mankind within. God lives in you and He lives in me through His Holy Spirit.

In the same way that the Son is a manifest expression of the Father and only ever did what the Father said and did, the Holy Spirit is the manifest expression of the Son and will only ever say or do what the Son would say or do. The Trinity is manifest operation. The perfect oneness and unity that They have is expressed in Their love for us.

While ministering in Nigeria, I stayed at an evangelist/pastor's home. His ministry was known throughout many counties for God's healing power flowing through him. He explained to me that the reason why miracles were so common with his ministry and among his people was that the Holy Spirit gave Him a revelation of how we should treat God's Word. He felt the Holy Spirit ask him to teach his people to not view God's Word as ancient or as a mere teaching tool, but that God stood behind His Word to perform His promises. If Jesus were to appear physically to you and say, "Rise and be healed", you would. Well, He is saying it to you through His Word. Apply faith to His promise and watch. Because of this understanding and childlike faith, great signs and wonders are occurring, causing God's Kingdom to be established in very dark places.

Jesus told his disciples to tarry in Jerusalem and wait until they received power from on high. That was HOLY SPIRIT POWER. The church was birthed in power and can only maintain and advance itself in HOLY SPIRIT POWER. Jesus' entire ministry was marked by His anointing as the Messiah/Christ, which was proven by the miracles, signs and wonders He performed. If Jesus functioned by the Spirit's impetus, how much more should you and I?

*Holy Spirit, You are welcome. Holy Spirit, You are welcome here in my life. Wind of Heaven blow over my life. Have Your way in me. Anoint me. Baptize me. Enable me.*

## Day 80

## I Am the Light of the World

[5] As long as I am in the world, I am the light of the world." John 9:5

If someone were to ask us what the light of the world is, most of us would answer, – "The sun." How could that be wrong? The most essential light, however, is not the one that hangs in the sky. There are a multitude of benefits that come from the sun, yet they pale in comparison to the ones we receive from the Son.

Acts 9 records what happened to Saul when Jesus "enlightened him". Jesus the Son shone brighter than the noonday sun, blinding Saul and turning him into Paul the great Apostle. The book of Revelation tells us that in heaven there will be no need of the sun or moon because the Lamb will be the light and there will be no night (Revelations 21:23-24).

Jesus is the illumination or revelation of all that life was intended to be. Without the revelation of who God is and why we were created, sighted people are blind and cannot see, no matter how much light they may have. It is those who come to God and acknowledge that they are blind and need to see from His perspective who truly have sight.

Jesus reiterated this truth when He healed the blind man and spoke to the religious leaders of His day. He readily told them that they were blind because they would not acknowledge their sinfulness.

Sin is the greatest blinding agent in the world. There is nothing else that can compare to it. It is little wonder that the Apostle Paul prays for the Ephesus Church so fervently that the eyes of their understanding would be enlightened or illuminated to understand God:

> **[15] This is why, since I heard about your faith in the Lord Jesus and your love for all the saints, [16] I never stop giving thanks for you as I remember you in my prayers. [17] I pray that the God of our Lord Jesus Christ, the glorious Father, would give you a spirit of wisdom and revelation in the knowledge of Him. [18] I pray that the perception**

**of your mind may be enlightened so you may know what is the hope of His calling, what are the glorious riches of His inheritance among the saints, [19] and what is the immeasurable greatness of His power to us who believe, according to the working of His vast strength.** Ephesians 1:15-19

Paul's prayer is a manifestation of our need to know that Jesus is the revelation and illuminator of truth, significance, purpose and glory. Paul's prayer is for wisdom, revelation, enlightenment, calling, purpose and of God's immeasurable power and inheritance made available to the believer. Jesus our Light is the One who illuminates these truths to us so that we can walk in the fulfillment God intended.

*Thank You, Lord Jesus, for illuminating the love of God to my heart for me and for the lost, for showing me I was created for the purpose of revealing Your glory. Thank You for purposing me to be a part of Your family, drawing wayward sons and daughters back home. Thank You for the power of the Holy Spirit residing in my life.*

## Day 81

### Jesus Meek and Lowly

**Read Matthew 11:29**

When you hear the phrase "meek and lowly in heart", what are the first words that come to your mind? Are they words commonly used to describe yourself or words commonly used to describe Jesus? The only character qualities that Jesus used to describe Himself in all His ministry are in Matthew 11:29. Humility and gentleness are the cornerstones of God's Kingdom. If Jesus used these words to describe Himself and our greatest aim in life is to like Him, then it only makes sense that God is calling us to be gentle and humble.

The Lord Jesus says to us, "Take my partnership and learn who I truly am and you will learn to be gentle and to be humble. You will be gentle in how you treat one another and honest on in the inside as to who I have made you to be. You will be fearless when it comes to expressing who you truly are and you will trust in the Father, knowing that He will work all things out for your good. You will be gentle because there is no one that you will ever meet who will not respond to My gentleness in you. So many people have been offended by a wrong representation of Me, but as you learn who I truly am, you will be able to be a true representation of Me. Meekness is not weakness; it is divine strength under divine control. Humility is not emptying oneself of worth and value and feeling useless, but instead it is knowing the great eternal value and worth that I have placed upon you and revelling in the truth of who I made you to be. Giving me glory and put your trust in Me in and through each and every situation I allow into your life."

The ultimate example of Jesus' meekness and humility was when He endured the trial under Pilate and the crucifixion itself. John 13:3 says, "Jesus knowing that the Father had given all things into his hands, and that he was come from God, and went to God rose and washed the feet of His disciples and declared to them that His time was come." Jesus was fully cognizant of who He was, where He was from and where He was going. Out of that strength and truth, He marched into Calvary and overcame for all time sin, death and hell.

*I am Yours, oh God. I came from You and, like Jesus, I will come back to You for eternity. My life here is to be filled with Your grace and love flowing out through me. Help me to always walk in gentleness and humility to Your glory and praise.*

## Day 82

### Jesus the Prophet

**"The things concerning Jesus the Nazarene, who was a Prophet powerful in action and speech before God and all the people"**, Luke 24:19

God is all-knowing. This is called "omniscience". All wisdom knowledge and understanding belong to Him, from the tiniest DNA strand too the largest planet in the universe. Nothing is outside of His sight or knowledge. This includes present knowledge, past knowledge and everything regarding the future.

Jesus, although so much more than a prophet, functioned fully within this office and calling of a prophet. He foretold future events, not only of His second coming but details concerning his death and resurrection. God knows all about everything before events take place. The Spirit of God that rested on Jesus showed Him things to come.

Our world is given over to supernatural phenomenon. On television, we see psychics, mediums and people who channel spirits openly functioning under demonic guides. The days are past where the believer can be devoid of power.

Jesus said to his disciples that they should wait in Jerusalem until power from on high would visit them. When the Holy Spirit fell on the day of Pentecost, 3000 people were saved and the ministry of the apostles and the disciples in the New Testament showed a continual outpouring of God's power. The answer to the influx of counterfeit power and spiritual experience is the authentic, true and righteous power of God.

Jesus is still baptizing His Church with the Holy Spirit, which we so desperately need to counter the sin and degradation of our day. One element of His presence in our lives is that the Holy Spirit will show us things to come. The same Spirit dwells in us and will fulfill the desire of God, which is as Moses said, that "all God's people were prophets". Numbers 11:29 As well, the Prophet Joel promises that "your sons and daughters shall prophesy" (Joel 2:28). We are a prophetic people and the reason that we are a prophetic people is because our God is a prophetic God. His Word is a prophetic Word. His Spirit cannot but speak of what is to come as a confirmation of God being God but also for the people of God to prepare for the fulfillment of all that God has spoken. The indwelling Spirit gives us words of wisdom and knowledge of events we could not otherwise know the accuracy of. What we say will be used by God to draw the lost to Christ (1 Corinthians 14:23-25).

God desires to show you His plans for your future, actual events that will take place in your life. Because you will be a witness for Him, He will release to you the Word of Wisdom and the Word of Knowledge as well as being prophetic, all for the purpose of drawing people into a saving relationship with Jesus Christ. We will look at these gifts more in depth when we discuss the Holy Spirit's activity.

*Holy Spirit have your way.*

## Week Three

1. When we reject the truths of God's word what in fact are we rejecting?
2. What is the greatest blinding agent in the world?
3. Why are Christians naturally a prophetic people?
4. Can you see the progression from disciples to servants and from servants to friends and then from friends to brothers as being significant? What does it mean to you that Jesus calls us brothers and leads us to Our Father?
5. Quote last week's memory verse and pick a new verse for the week.

## Day 83

### The Lion of the Tribe of Judah

**Then one of the elders said to me, "Stop crying. Look! The Lion from the tribe of Judah, the Root of David, has been victorious so that He may open the scroll and its seven seals." Then I saw One like a slaughtered lamb standing between the throne and the four living creatures and among the elders. He had seven horns and seven eyes, which are the seven spirits of God sent into all the earth.** Revelation 5:5-6

Let's take a minute and consider these two revelations of God as two different sides of an equation. If we were to insert an equal sign here we would have a very difficult time saying that a Lion = a Lamb or that a Lamb = a Lion. If we were to play a word association game and the word "Lion" was given to us, "Lamb" would not be the first thought that would come to our mind and vice versa.

In the eternal Kingdom of God, the Lamb of God is also the Lion of the tribe of Praise and the Lion of the tribe of Praise is also the Lamb of God. C.S. Lewis' depiction of Jesus as Aslan/the lion who willingly laid down his life and rose again was intriguing. We see here a revelation of the heart of God himself for us, for as He loved us so much and was willing to die in our place, He is forever acknowledged in Heaven as the only One worthy to open the sealed books of God's judgment. No other being in the universe could be found worthy to open the book of God's coming plan and purposes of the ages, but the One who paid the price of redemption.

Now He laid down His life as the Lamb or God, but He is also the Captain of Angel Armies and of the Church Army on the earth. As the Lion of the tribe of Praise, He is absolutely feared and sends terror in the hearts of the enemy.

Hunters from around the world will tell you when they are hunting lions that, when they hear its majestic roar, they are dumbstruck with fear. Many tremble and lose heart; others overcome their fear and continue the hunt.

This is not the case when Jesus roars from Heaven. All of His enemies tremble and pray for the mountains to fall on them in fear of His judgment. Please note in the scripture that it refers to Jesus as the Lamb bringing judgment, for it is the rejection of the Lamb's perfect sacrifice that seals our judgment. It is the goodness of God that leads us to repentance that we reject and incur the wrath of God (Revelations 6:15-17).

If Jesus the Son of God, in His character and person, was personified as both lamb and lion there will be aspects of this same nature that will be revealed in our own lives. Lamb, servant and love slave to God and to His people, but also a lion nature that causes the ruler, overcomer, king within me to conquer sin and the works of the enemy. God is working to produce both natures in us. We get it wrong when we use our ruling nature with people and our servant nature with sin. Christ came to realign us to God's perfect plan, to be overcomers through serving in righteousness and to be overcomers in defeating the darkness.

*Perfect Creator, Eternal God, my King and my Daddy, I so wish to approach my life in this perfect balance that You made me to have. Help me to be ever mindful of ruling in life through laying down my life for others and ruling in life by overcoming all the powers of the enemy. I know that, like Jesus, You will move through me to accomplish Your perfect will in every situation.*

## Day 84

### Jesus is My Daily Bread

**So Jesus said to them, "I assure you: Unless you eat the flesh of the Son of Man and drink His blood, you do not have life in yourselves.** John 6:45

**Taste and see that the Lord is good**. Psalm 34:8

When I was a teenager, a California mom came up with a novel idea. First of all she had the most delectable cookie known to mankind, one that upon tasting, you couldn't help but shut your eyes and say, "Mmm, mmm, mmm, mmmmm, mmmmmmmmmm." Yeah, one of those cookies. To make matters worse, the cookies were cooked on the premises so the wafting odour would draw you in like Bugs Bunny to carrots or a dog to a bone. Now, some marketing executive said, "Let's take it a step further." So he had stores on street corners rigged with doors that would open as you walked by and, when you were hit with the smell of those cookies, it was game over.

Food has always been one of mankind's weak points. We all need food to survive, so metaphors with food in them are universally accepted. So when God says that man shall not live by bread alone, it does not take long for us to figure out that our natural food can never give us spiritual satisfaction or fulfillment. But if we live in obedience to God's Word, we will have ultimate satisfaction and fulfillment. Now Jesus in this scripture before us blew the minds of His listeners. He said, "If you don't eat my flesh and drink my blood, you will have no relationship with Me." Although this is clearly a reference to the communion table and the revelation of Christ on the cross, there is more to what Jesus was saying than placing the fulfillment of this command in the Table of the Lord. This is a topic loaded with spiritual truths that we will try and scratch the surface on in another series.

Eat Me, drink Me or have nothing to do with Me. Food is to the natural man what God is to our spiritual man. If you go without natural food, you die; if you go without the presence of God in your life, you die. The better the food that you eat, the stronger you are; the more time in the presence of God, living in obedience to Him, the more of an overcomer you will be. Food gives nutrients, minerals and vitamins that are a total benefit to our physical bodies as well as to our longevity.

If we eat the wrong food, we actually can cause many sicknesses that can lead to death and a much shorter lifespan.

Our spirit needs God more than our bodies need food. God is meant to be experienced. It is not enough to know about God, to be filled with great theology but have no experience of His personhood. The greatest day in my life was my salvation day, the day God called me by name and the revelation of His love for me changed my life. Almost forty years later, I still get teary eyed when I think about it, God loved a wretch like me, sent His own Son to die in my place and opened heaven not just so that I could have eternal life, but that I might have a love relationship with the God of the universe. To not experience His love, but to know it was there would be hell.

God has pursued us in salvation; now it is our turn to pursue Him. I want to apprehend the apprehender. He captured my heart; now I want to capture His. Think about the statement, "You are what you eat." What are you eating? What are you feeding on?

You cannot give what you do not have. Peter said, "Silver and gold, I don't have, but what I do have I give to you. In the name of Jesus of Nazareth, get up and walk (Acts 3:6). Peter had learned to ingest God, to have Him living on the inside and mightily moving on the outside. God desires this for all of his children. We must choose to feed on God's goodness and presence.

*Lord, Your Word is filled with the truth that You are everything that we need for fulfillment and joy in life. True contentment comes from godliness. I choose You, Lord above all else. I run to You each and every day for the strength and grace I need to live my life.*

## Day 85

### The King of Israel

**Took branches of palm trees, and went forth to meet him, and cried, Hosanna: Blessed is the King of Israel that cometh in the name of the Lord.** Matthew 21:8, 9

When God spoke to Abraham, He told him that his seed would be like the stars of the sky and like the sand of the sea. At the time, Abraham did not even have one descendant. Though his name was great and he had great wealth, he had no heir. This promise would have seemed impossible when one considers that his wife was also barren. But God's promise to Abraham was fulfilled.

There were two distinct groups of people that came from Abraham: a people of his race (a national people) and a people of his faith (a spiritual people). Abraham's grandson was named Jacob, but a time came in his life in which his name was changed from Jacob to Israel. He had a conversion experience, a transformation experience where his character was changed because of an encounter with God (Genesis 32:22-31). He went from being the natural son of Abraham to being the spiritual son of Abraham. He went from being a thief to a prince that has power with man and God, an overcomer.

Israel became the national name of Abraham's descendants, but it is not a foregone conclusion that one who is a physical descendant of Abraham is also a spiritual son of Abraham. In other words, nationality does not equal spirituality and will never equate to acceptance with God. One does not enter the Kingdom of God by natural birth but by spiritual birth. Jesus Himself says to Nicodemus, "You must be born again, or born from above to enter the Kingdom of God" (John 3:7). God is no respecter of persons, nationally. Fret not. I know of His promises to the seed of Abraham, but we must first recognize that national Israel must become spiritual Israel to be right with God.

When Jesus is called the King of Israel, we must be able to differentiate between Him being the King over spiritual Israel, the true people of God, and being King of the Jews (we will look at this tomorrow). Spiritual Israel is comprised of believers in every nation, from every tribe and tongue and ethnic group. It is not a natural distinction, but a spiritual distinction. It consists of those who have named

Christ as Lord, who also acknowledge Him as King of Israel, King of righteousness, King of Peace, King of the Jews, King of Glory, King of Heaven and the King of all Kings. He is the true King of their lives and they bow down to and seek to not only please Him in all things, but also to extend His Kingdom in the earth. This starts in our hearts and finds full expression in how we live our lives. We like Jacob of old have been transformed from within. Our nature has been changed and we are marked by His name.

*King of my heart I bow down to You. Is it any wonder that the wise men came bearing gifts to the One born King of the Jews? I give to You what is already owed to You: my life, and my all. May I be a willing sacrifice who does not seek to get up off of Your altar, but willingly lay down my life out of love for You.*

## Day 86

### King of the Jews

**And set up over his head his accusation written, THIS IS JESUS THE KING OF THE JEWS.** Matthew 27:37

Most people by now are aware that Jesus was born King of the Jews. Part of the reason that Herod sought Him out was he felt threatened by the knowledge that the prophets had declared that the true King of the Jews was being born. Now, we are talking about a racial king, the king that was prophesied about to Abraham and to David. God had said that from Abraham's line wold come kings and queens. In His covenant that He made with David, He said that there would never *not* be a King to rule from his lineage. Jesus, through both Joseph's line and Mary's line, had the genealogy to be King of the Jews. As common and ordinary as Mary and Joseph were, their children were all heirs to King David's throne.

Jesus was and is heir to what we term the "Throne of David". He was the rightful King over the Jewish people and He came so that the very plan of redemption might be fulfilled. God is the initiator of the nation of Israel and the Jewish people for the specific holy purpose of bringing His Son to earth to die in our place. The Jewish nation has suffered much because of their connection to the plan and purposes of God. We are sovereignly connected to them and they are sovereignly connected to us. In Romans, Paul describes us being grafted in to the olive tree, as well as the prophetic promises of God that in one day all Israel will be saved (Romans 14).

The rejection of Jesus as Israel's King and Messiah opened the door for the Gospel to go to the nations. Their future acceptance of Him will open the door to the end of the ages. How grateful we must be that God has opened our eyes to see Jesus for who He is and always will be! I am so glad that my eyes have been opened and I see King Jesus revealing the truth of who He is to my heart and through my life. For those who do not yet know Him and for the Jewish nation in particular, let our intercession ascend to God with gratitude and compassion for the harvest that God has promised (Isaiah 62:1).

The lives of the disciples and apostles give evidence to how committed and dedicated to Jesus as their Master, King and Potentate. They laid down their lives for the extension of His Kingdom. They were so in love with Him and with the message God had given them to carry. Jesus came preaching the Kingdom of God was at hand, most assuredly for the King of that Kingdom was within their very reach. In that He has called you and commissioned you, know for a fact that all of heaven's resources at your disposal to carry out the desires of the King.

*King Jesus, I bow down and worship You. There is none who can compare with You. Nothing on earth or in the universe can compare to You. I gladly submit my life to You and glory in being obedient to whatever You ask of me. I pray for those I am sharing Your love with. I pray that their hearts would be receptive to the truth of who You are and that You would open their hearts to the great price You paid for them.*

## Day 87

### I Am the Vine

**"I am the vine; you are the branches. The one who remains in Me and I in him produces much fruit, because you can do nothing without Me."** John 15:5

The main vine stock does not carry the grapes; it is the branches that do. The main vine stock carries the sap, the nutrients, and the life that enables the branches to flower and produce edible fruit. Any branch that is broken off from the stock will perish and die. Likewise, our connection to Christ is the means whereby our lives will produce fruit that will last. It is not in our inherent ability that we can do anything of value for the Kingdom, but what Christ completed on the cross and now does through us as we put our trust in Him.

The word to abide or remain is the Greek word *meno* and it means "to stay" (in a given place, state, relation or expectancy)12.. Jesus calls us to stay in faith in Him to do the work that He promised to do. It is never about what we can do, but it is always about what He can and will do through us. Remaining in total dependence, trust and faith in Him unlocks heavens doors to blessing and fruitfulness.

The state that God expects us to stay in is one of humility and dependence. This is the state that brought us to Christ in the first place; we came to an end of ourselves and realized that we could never save ourselves. Only Jesus could save us from our sins. We put our absolute trust and faith in the finished work of Calvary and believed and proclaimed Christ as Saviour and Lord. This is the doorway to all the miracles and power of God in our lives. Our status is one of loving humility and dependence on what Jesus has accomplished, knowing His love never changes.

When I think about the cross and what Jesus did for me, I cannot help but be moved to praise, worship and thanksgiving. The wonderful thing about a heart attitude of thanksgiving and praise is that it ushers us into the very presence of God. This is where God desires all of His children to abide. Our perspectives are purified there. Our eyes see clearly there. We see from our position seated in heavenly places in Christ Jesus. Our decisions are based not on what we feel but on who we are in Christ and who He is in us.

Our expectancy is one of faith in the truth that the promises of God are yes and amen. God is not a man that He should lie and Christ died so that we might have abundant life. Faith and expectancy really are intertwined. True faith has within it a divine expectation of blessing and divine visitation. True expectation will lead us to a place of faith and hope in God's willingness and desire to bless, love, heal and restore. The greater our expectancy is, the greater our faith will be. From this place of abiding faith in Christ, fruitfulness will flow, both in character and in an effective presentation of the gospel to those who do not know the Lord.

*I choose to abide in You Lord by praying without ceasing; worshipping You at all times, which will be the fruit of my lips giving praise to You; and meditating on Your written Word and on the words that Your Holy Spirit speaks into my heart in the highways and byways of life. I choose to abide in You. When my mind wants to wander, I choose to turn it back on Your grace and love. I choose an overcomer's mindset that with God on my side I am assured victory. Greater are You who is with me, than the enemy in the world.*

12. Thayer and Smith. "Greek Lexicon entry for Meno". "The NAS New Testament Greek Lexicon". . 1999.

## Day 88

### Prince of Peace

**I have told you these things so that in Me you may have peace. You will have suffering in this world. Be courageous! I have conquered the world."** John 16:33

Peace is one of those great Bible words. It is one of those words that when you hear it with understanding that your heart immediately responds and says, "I'll take that." The Hebrew word for peace is *shalom*. This is the word that Jesus is referring to when He says, "In me you have peace." The word *shalom* means wholeness and healing in your spirit, soul and body, safety, prosperity, tranquility, contentment, peace in your family and in your friendships, peace with God through covenant relationships and peace meaning the absence of war.13. I heard Pastor Bill Johnson mention this word in a message and said that it correlates to the Greek word "sozo", which comprises salvation, healing and deliverance for one's spirit, soul and body. Yes, it is like heaven on earth, the very thing that Jesus taught us to pray to come in His model prayer.

In Romans 15:17, the apostle Paul summed up the kingdom of God to be righteousness, peace and joy in the Holy Ghost. Peace is a fruit of the Spirit and, therefore, will grow in our lives as we cultivate it correctly. The Lord Jesus tells us that peace is only found in one place. We find it in Him. Romans 5 teaches us that it is a by-product of our right standing with God. The cross gives us Christ's righteousness. When you are in right standing with God, the automatic heart response is peace and contentment.

God, as the perfect Father, can only desire wholeness for His children. Do you know of any Father who would desire less for His child? When I know the love of God for me, then I begin to walk down the road of wholeness in my soul, my mind and my emotions.

If there is anything that we must guard against in life, it is the loss of our peace with God. Jesus promised that if we would stay in Him, our peace would be intact. It is when we fail to guard against sin that we lose our peace and, like Adam and Eve, we try to cover ourselves with fig leaves (our righteousness instead of His righteousness).

Guard your peace and guard your joy by staying on guard against sin in your life. The norm for a Christian is to be filled to overflowing with peace and joy because of our right standing before God. The more we live God's way, the greater the release of His peace and joy in our lives. When they are not present, it is a warning sign that we have moved away from the secret place and must get back to rejoicing in His love and favor in our lives through the cross.

Daddy, I choose to live in Your glorious and wonderful peace, I have experienced it and I cannot even put into words the wholeness and the contentment I know because I am in right standing with You. I choose to live here ......I arm myself with a heart of obedience and humility that I might live in Your joyous peace.

13. http://www.therefinersfire.org/meaning_of_shalom.htm

## Day 89

### Water and the Rock

**"Take the staff you used to strike the Nile. And go. I'm going to be present before you there on the rock at Horeb. You are to strike the rock. Water will gush out of it and the people will drink.**" (Exodus 17: 6 The Message)

**They drank from the Rock, God's fountain for them that stayed with them wherever they were. And the Rock was Christ.**1 Cor. 10:4

Jesus Christ was God's fountain for Israel and Jesus Christ is God's fountain for you and for me. The difference is obvious, in that it was a literal rock, with natural water in the Old Testament that Christ revealed Himself through in type and shadow, but in the New Testament He is a literal person but spiritual water. Now there is very real implication from 1 Corinthians 10:4 interpreting the Old Testament Scriptures that God through Christ literally travelled with the nation of Israel, not only in the Cloud by day and the Pillar of Fire by night but as a Rock that looked like any other Rock but was indeed Christ with them, watching over them and providing for them.

It is on the cross that this is so powerfully fulfilled. For they did indeed strike Him and blood and water flowed from His side. Although that water was literal, it more powerfully speaks to the water of life that He so freely provides that gives life to us all.

David proclaimed in the most famous of Psalms, "He leads me beside still waters." We are made in such a way that fulfillment in life cannot come from anything other than from God Himself. Billy Graham described it as a "God-shaped vacuum inside each of us that only God can fill". Not only does God desire to fill us with Himself, He wants to baptize us and overflow us with Himself continually. (We will look at this more when we look at the Person of the Holy Spirit.) Ephesians 5 tells us to be continually filled to overflowing with the Holy Spirit. Jesus said out of our belly would flow rivers of living water, which gives the picture of an artesian well living on the inside of us providing unlimited life-giving resources. I don't know about you, but that sounds mighty good to me!

You can see Paul and Silas in prison. They had just been whipped and they are black and blue and bloodied, and yet when others would be angry, cursing and maybe even second guessing their commitment, Paul and Silas sang praises at midnight. They tapped into life, tapped into grace, tapped into power to overcome. Their hearts were right before God. They had no time for a pity party, only time for a Holy Ghost party, and boy did it come! An earthquake came and shook them free and ended with more people being added to the kingdom. If they could praise Him through that, a circumstance most of us will never endure, I know we have a lot of tapping into to do. God's life has been made available to us but too many times we look to other things to satisfy and fulfill us and they simply will not do.

*Daddy, my life has been transformed by You. I have a joy and a peace that I never knew before. It is clear to me that the more I am in Your presence, the greater the flow of Your life in me and through me. The greater the joy and the peace I have. I choose to live in the water of Your love more and more so I can be more like You.*

## Day 90

## The Rod That Budded

**The next day Moses entered the tent of the testimony and saw that Aaron's staff, representing the house of Levi, had sprouted, formed buds, blossomed, and produced almonds!** Numbers 17:8

We end this section with a prophetic picture given through a symbol that took place in the history of Israel. Moses and Aaron were God-ordained leadership, but there were those who rebelled against them because they wanted to take on that role themselves. There was both jealousy and envy in their hearts that fed the rebellion to the point where they rose up and actually gathered a following to almost make a coup of God's leaders.

God was not pleased and intervened. He set out a test to show who he had ordained. Dead sticks were chosen and placed before the presence of The Lord, each representing a specific tribe of Israel. When they came in the next morning one rod (Aaron's rod) was not like the other rods.

Numbers 17:8 shows us the rod in an amazing state, for what was dead was now alive. This theme is a central theme throughout the scriptures in numerous situations. It all leads up to the greatest and most significant resurrection of all– Jesus Christ, the Lord of Glory, laying down His life for us and being raised from the dead.

What sets Jesus apart from all other religious leaders is not only His words, His power and His sacrifice but the fact that He conquered death. No other religious leader even makes such a claim. God shows that He approves of Christ's sacrifice by raising Him from the dead. It is no wonder that the scriptures insist that there is no other name given under heaven whereby we must be saved (Acts 4:12). Jesus is the ultimate fulfillment of the Rod that Budded. That which was dead has come back to life.

The story of Aaron's rod also speaks of God ordained leadership. All authority is ordained by God. Romans 13:1 tells us, "It is not something to be grasped or something to fight against." The leader is chosen by God, not because they are loved more by God or because they have a greater value. No, it is because God has a plan and a purpose of each of us and not all can be called as leaders.

The leader that is called is called by divine appointment. There is a miraculous element involved in the choosing, placing and installing of a spiritual leader into the role that God has for them. Ask any leader the process that God has taken them through and you find miracle after miracle following their footsteps, showing the hand of God upon their lives. Scripture is replete with God calling and choosing leaders while they were still in the womb. God planned and purposed them for His work in the earth.

You cannot make yourself be called if you are not called to leadership. Are all called? Yes. Do we all have certain areas in our lives where we are called to lead and to be leaders? Yes. But there are specific calls to leadership that are divinely chosen and are evidenced by the confirming work of God in their lives and ministry.

Bill Johnson commented on the four stages of the rod that budded being a picture of the life of a leader. No earthly man is perfect and every leader is being molded and shaped by God into the image and likeness of Christ, even as every believer is. They are in process even as we are in process, but you will be able to look at their lives and see fruit like the almonds fully grown on the rod. You will see gifting that is burgeoning and preparing to come into its final stages like a flower blossomed. You will see buds of development areas that need some work and growth. They are not all that they could be but are in process. You can see sprout of things God is just starting to work on and that will be finished in God's season. This speaks volumes to me for Aaron was surely in that state. Scripture records failures in his life that we would never want in the life of a leader in our life, and yet He was chosen and ordained of God to lead and God defended him to the death.

Honor, pray for, respect and submit to the leaders God has placed in your life. They work for God and for your good. Make it easy for them.

*Daddy, You established leaders to be a blessing in my life and to work with You in developing me into the child of God that You have called me to be. I submit to You by my submission to them. Forgive me for thoughts of rebellion or angst as You are sharpening me through them. I pray Your great blessing and provision on their lives. Multiply the anointing on them. I understand they are in process and You did not call them because they were perfect. You called them to demonstrate who You are and to bless the earth with who You are in many different ways. I honor You in how I honor them. Bless my pastors Lord, I pray.*

## Day 91

### Happiest Man Ever

**Your throne, O God, *is* forever and ever; A scepter of righteousness *is* the scepter of Your kingdom.**
**7 You love righteousness and hate wickedness; Therefore God, Your God, has anointed You**
**With the oil of gladness more than Your companions**. Psalm 45:6,7

As we continue our exploration of who our Saviour is, we gain revelation and insight as we come to the Word of God. Jesus down through history would have been described as a "man of sorrows", for truly the Word of God declares Him as such. We see Him weeping in His earthly ministry (though we should note that the God who made emotion is not directed by them but instead, being perfect, reveals the perfect emotional response in every situation).

God the Father has anointing that He desires to give to us, the richest gift that one can ever receive. There is nothing on earth that can compare to the various ordinations that God desires to give—anointing for ministry, for prophecy, for healing, for deliverance and more. But in considering these, many of us might miss the one that Psalm 45:6 describes. That is an anointing with the oil of gladness of Spirit of Joy.

It is said here that Jesus was the happiest man on planet earth. There was no one filled with greater joy or a bigger smile. Though that may not be how He is portrayed in history or in art, God gave Him this anointing because of His perfect balance in the most important of issues. Jesus loved righteousness and hated wickedness. It is for this reason alone that He was filled with unmistakeable joy and peace.

If you love something, you yearn for it, treasure it, protect it, share it and, in any way possible, see that it is increased. The opposite would be said for something that you hate. You would reject it, detest it, defeat it, ensure that it is limited and try to remove it with all determination. Think of sin and what it has brought to the planet, what it has done in bringing death, sickness, disease, depression, sadness, grief, oh how long the list. Remove sin and you remove all this.

King Jesus lived to eradicate sin and its consequences. He did this by loving and pursuing righteousness, by healing, by delivering, by discipling, by blessing others and by sacrificing His own life. God the Father looking down and seeing this overflowed Him with "joy unspeakable and full of glory". Jesus had an infectious radical joy in His heart and the reason for it is His heart was rest in His Father's love for Him. Want more joy? Love what is right, hate what is evil and live your life revealing it and you already know the outcome (Acts 10:38).

*Daddy, I so look forward to knowing You more and releasing Your perspective and insight to a world that simply does not who You truly are. Reveal Yourself more and more through my life.*

## Week Four

1. What does true faith have within it?
2. What do our spirits need more than our bodies need food?
3. What did Paul and Silas tap into while in prison and how did they do it?
4. What caused Jesus to be the happiest, most joy filled person on earth?
5. Why is Jesus Christ your King?
6. Quote last week's memory verse and memorize Exodus 3:14

## Day 92

## The Word of Direction

**Thy word is a lamp unto my feet, and a light unto my path.** Psalm 119:105

We are now into our fourth month of our devotional. There are a number of factors that contribute to how you view the Word of God. As you have been growing, truth is coming into your life on a daily basis because of the attention that you're paying to the Word of God in your life. Over the next 30 days, we're going to take some time and look more intently into how God uses His Word to transform our lives.

I will not take the time to go into the history of how we got what we term "the Bible". Though we live in a day in which many people say the Bible cannot be taken literally or has any form of life to be followed, we are also seeing numerous other books being treated as though they are equal to the Word of God. The Word of God declares the Bible alone is God's Word to man. It also warns us that if we add anything to it, God will add to our judgment and if we take anything out of it, He will remove our name out of His book.

The scripture before us declares that the Word of God is both a lamp and a light to our lives. I don't know about you, but at first that might seem strange. Why do I need two different light sources to enable me to get from point A to point B? But if we pause but for a moment and take a closer look, we can see the significance of these varied light sources in our daily lives.

The first and most significant light that we embrace and enjoy is the light that comes from the sun. Through that light God gives life to everything in the earth and enables us to see clearly and to rejoice in the glory of God's creation. For long distance and for getting clear vision for what is ahead, the light of the sun is perfect. In daytime, even in difficult places the sunlight is more than adequate.

We can draw the parallels concerning the Word of God. God's Word is an overshadowing, all-encompassing, fully exposing light to the realities of what life is about. We need that light for it enables us to have understanding, wisdom and knowledge concerning the fullest dimensions of what God intended life to be about. Without that light, we are in true darkness.

We also need a lamp to direct us as we are about to take steps in to many areas of life that we have not been before. A lamp would have been carried in the hand and therefore would have been close to the feet. It would light the path of someone who was walking in a dark place. There are times in our lives when we need to make decisions and it can be confusing or difficult to figure out what is the best or most beneficial step to take. Through the examples and clear teaching of the Word of God we have principles available to us to enable us to make decisions that lead us out of danger, away from detours and perfectly on track to what God has for us. That is why we have the Word of God available to us—to lead us and guide the decision-making process and to assure us that our decision will be pleasing to God.

*Father, I thank You for Your Word of God that is transforming my life. Let a greater hunger for truth be in my heart to take in all that You have for me from Your Word. Give me a love for Your Word, that it would be more important to me than my breath and my daily bread. Give me a yearning for truth, which Jesus declared was Your Word (John 17:17).*

## Day 93

## Religion vs. Relationship

**Jesus said, "You're way off base, and here's why: One, you don't know your Bibles; two, you don't know how God works.** Mark 12:24

**" So faith comes from what is heard, and what is heard comes through the message about Christ"** Romans 10:17

Have you ever noticed that when you're reading the Word of God, reading Christian material or listening to a sermon that there are certain texts that leap out and grab you? You know for a fact that God is speaking to you. What happens at that very instant, in that second, is the opportunity for faith to be attached to what God is speaking to you about.

There are two primary Greek words used to describe our word for a "word". One is *logos* and the other is *rhema.* There are different nuances to go with these two words but the one that we want to look at today and relate to our lives more is the word *rhema.*

In Mark 12 as mentioned above some Sadducees came to Jesus and asked him a very theological question. The strange thing is that they did not even believe in the afterlife. Jesus explains why they were unable to comprehend the truths He was giving, for they did not know "the scriptures" and they did not know the "power of God". Most of these men would have memorized the entire Pentateuch by the time they were twelve years old. So how could they do not know their Bibles?

They knew the literal words, but not to what those words were speaking about. They knew the words in their heads but the words were not life-giving to their spirit and so, in their hearts, they could not apply faith to what they truly did not believe. Jesus went on to say that they did not know God's power and yet the scripture is a revelation of the power of God.

The danger for all of us is in a walk with God is that we can know about Him, and yet not truly know Him. We can tell people all kinds of facts and figures about God but not give them God.

It is like reading a biography about Abraham Lincoln or Martin Luther King Jr. We can know their likes and dislikes, birthdays and anniversaries. We can be scholars on their lives and yet never really know them. A person who knew them by experience would always have a greater relationship and would be more able to reveal who they truly were.

What keeps us ever growing and maturing and relevant is that we not only hear from God through a rhema but that we obey what God says to us. God has purposed that we make the scriptures come alive in our life and times, that the same God of the Bible turn the world upside down because we are experiencing Him and we enable others to experience Him as well. That can only happen as we both know the scriptures and the power (the Holy Spirit). Religion will never replace relationship, all the talk of having a relationship with God pales in comparison to actually having one.

*Father, my prayer to You is that my heart would ever be responsive to Your Word. When You speak to me, I will not explain it away but, with childlike faith, I will receive and experience more and more of You enabling me to be a world changer.*

## Day 94

## Living on The Word

**But He answered, "It is written: Man must not live on bread alone but on every word that comes from the mouth of God."** Matthew 4:4

Jesus was tempted by the enemy during a time of fasting. One of the temptations was that Jesus would turn stones into bread and then eat it, meeting His most basic need. Jesus responded to the enemy with the verse that is before us today.

Jesus was seeking His Father. He was out in the desert fasting and preparing for the new stage of ministry that God the Father had for him. The adversary came when Jesus was at his weakest in the natural and he knew that Jesus would desperately need food. He had seen how mankind throughout history had always put his natural desires before his spiritual desires. Adam made that mistake with Eve in the Garden of Eden when he failed the test of the eyes and the test of the flesh. Adam failed to obey the known revealed will of God to satisfy the desires of experiential knowledge and physical satisfaction. Now the Son of God, as the Second Adam, is enduring a very similar temptation, but He rightly discerns the ramifications and sets the stage for all of us in how to overcome the enemy. Jesus responded by quoting from the book of Deuteronomy, which is the "book of remembrance".

Man's life will never be fulfilled by simply fulfilling the natural desires of the body; man's life can only be fulfilled by a living on the Word of God. Fulfillment in life comes from a right relationship with God and not anything else. Every time we try and fill the God-shaped vacuum in our hearts with something other than God, we end up barren and famished.

Does it not make sense that we would find our fulfillment in life from our source of life? With all that God created for us to enjoy and to take pleasure in, none of those things can or should ever take His place. But due to our sinfulness we constantly are trying to find fulfillment in life outside of our love affair with our Maker.

Jesus words here cut through all time and eternity and declare once and for all that our fulfillment in life comes from our source of life which is the very Word of God. We owe our very existence to the Word of God, for God spoke our lives into existence. Jesus is declared to be the very Word of God who was the instrument the Father used to bring us into being. God's Word, the person of

Jesus, is where we find our complete nourishment, satisfaction, joy and healing. No steak dinner can ever do that, no matter how triple AAA it may be. Every natural need/desire will only cry out to be met again and again. Their fulfillment is transitory; the fulfillment that God brings is eternal. The more of God we have, the more fulfillment we have in our lives. The opposite is also true as well. The less of God we have, the less of fulfillment and true meaning we have in our lives.

Let the Word of God fuel you and you will overflow with an ever continual wellspring of life.

## Day 95

### Faith Enables The Miraculous

**So faith comes by hearing [what is told], and what is heard comes by the preaching [of the message that came from the lips] of Christ (the Messiah Himself).** Romans 10:17 Amplified

**Before you trust, you have to listen. But unless Christ's Word is preached, there's nothing to listen to.** Romans 10:17 The Message

Let me tell you a personal story. I was ministering in Nigeria away from my wife and two children. My wife had just undergone radiation therapy because she had thyroid cancer. We had believed God to heal her and had anointed her neck with oil for thirty days, for that is all the time we had from the diagnosis to the medical procedure. After ten days or so in Nigeria, I was able to call my wife. Instead of the normal pleasantries, my wife got right down to business and told me "I was three days pregnant when I ingested the radiation pill. There is no hope for the baby. They are begging me to take the abortion pill, but I have refused. The Holy Spirit has spoken to my heart that everything is going to be ok."

I choked up immediately and changed the subject, asked to speak to my other children, felt the pressure of the line-up of people behind me wanting the phone, told my wife I loved her and that we would stand on God's word for a miracle. I was devastated internally, trying to hold back tears in front of the new minister whom I was to minister for. We drove for five or six hours in the West African heat to his home where I ran to my room to cried out to God.

From a teenager, I had believed God for an Isaac. In prayer I felt the sovereign God of heaven challenge my heart, that this was my Isaac and to turn to Genesis 18 and reread the story. I refused for at least thirty minutes, arguing that I was setting myself up for a happy ending, because of how well I knew the scriptures. I knew what was in Genesis 18. It is one of my favorite stories in the Bible because of the communion between God and Abraham. I repented and turned and was overwhelmed not with the story, but with a rhema – a message from the lips of Christ - that there is nothing too wonderful, marvelous or extraordinary for God to accomplish on your behalf. God directed my heart to two other miraculous births where this word is used and FAITH leapt within my heart to believe. Isaac, as of March 31, 2013 is thirteen years old and is a “medical miracle”.

My point is the process of faith that takes place in our hearts and lives as we pay attention to the Holy Spirit's voice. Had God not come and breathed life into my spirit by speaking to me a rhema word, a living Word from the lips of Christ, which in this case was also an application of a word from the scriptures, I would have floundered, claiming numerous verses to put my faith in. But God had a living word for me that was intimate, personal and perfectly fitted to our relationship. He desires to do the same for all of His children. He is not a respecter of persons.

*Pray as you feel led.*

## Day 96

## Sharper than Samurai Sword or Jedi Saber

**"For the word of God is living and effective and sharper than any double-edged sword, penetrating as far as the separation of soul and spirit, joints and marrow. It is able to judge the ideas and thoughts of the heart"** Hebrews 4:12

No other book that has been written or will be written can be compared to the Word of God. The first of many reasons is that the Word of God is alive, for the Person who spoke it is still alive and still echoing these words that will never die. The psalmist says God's word is established in the heavens for eternity (Psalm 119:89). Jesus said His word would never ever pass away (Matthew 24:35). Only God is able to back up every word that He has ever spoken. No man can ever say that.

When Jesus spoke with people, He would always go to the very heart of the matter. He never allowed what was happening on the surface of a situation to distract Him from the very source issue. In John 3, when Nicodemus came to Jesus calling Him a "good teacher", Jesus went right into the issue of being born again, answering the unspoken question of Nicodemus' heart. When Jesus was at a Pharisee's house, Jesus, discerning his heart, said to him, "May I ask you a question and then he proceeded to convict the Pharisee that his love was lukewarm instead of a blazing fire. Jesus shows us that those who are truly forgiven will respond with lavish love and worship for the forgiveness that they have received?" (Luke 7:36-50). When Jesus released the prostitute from being stoned, He did it with a word that cut to the heart of all those with stones in their hands (John 8:1-6). The prophet Isaiah declared that the Messiah would "delight in the fear of the Lord. He will not judge by what He sees with His eyes, He will not execute justice by what He hears with His ears" (Isaiah 11:3).His judgment will be in the Spirit; His words will go to the heart and open up the heavens to those He ministers to.

There are numerous examples of how the words of Jesus would cut to the very core issues of one's life to bring conviction, healing or deliverance. When we come to God's Word each day, we must be prepared and even invite the Holy Spirit to bring conviction into our lives in areas which He is putting His finger for us to repent of or release. Our openness and obedience will produce the process of maturity in our lives.

The other side of this is when we share the Word of God with others; it will do a similar work in them. God is at work in His Word to transform and shape lives. Whether as seed being sown into an unbeliever's life for a future harvest or as a word of correction or encouragement in a believer's life, God's word can never return unproductive (Isaiah 55:11).

Living Word, there is an aspect of change and maturity that I am looking for in my life. I want to be more like YOU and I know that this can only happen as I embrace the work of YOUR living Word showing me the path that I must take. The glorious truth is that as I embrace who I am in YOU I am empowered to be more like YOU. I choose to embrace the process of change through the sword of YOUR WORD.

## Day 97

## The Map of Your Word

**How shall a young man cleanse his way? By taking heed *and* keeping watch [on himself] according to Your word [conforming his life to it.** Psalm 119:9 Amplified

When Christ comes to live on the inside of us, we have an instant desire to please God with our whole lives. We seek to live holy lives, conquering sin as God highlights different areas of our character that we need to focus on.

David was confronted with a giant that desired to instill fear in all of Israel. David, in faith, won the day, but even though Goliath fell down dead, David took an extra step by taking Goliath's sword and cutting off his head. A simple message: take the extra step and make doubly sure that the sin you are facing is put to death. This spiritual principle, when followed, will result in the blessing of God in your life. When it is not put into practice, you will have constant difficulty overcoming.

As I have grown into manhood, one of the things that I absolutely love is going places where I have never been before. I so enjoy using Google maps or a good old fashioned map book for mapping out my journey. As I get into the car and begin the journey, I am usually giddy with excitement because I know that I am being led and directed by God into this mini adventure, which means He has a plan and a purpose for it. I have been blessed to have some rather extensive journeys that have crossed oceans to fulfill His plans and purposes for my life. Maps don't work so well in those instances, but the excitement and gratitude is there usually exponentially.

Many people if they would be honest would say, "If life has a road map, give it to me. I need it." Well, thankfully, there is a road map and you probably hold it in your hands or just did. God's Word is the ultimate roadmap to living a fulfilled, godly and Christ-pleasing life. The book of Proverbs declared that the beginning of all wisdom is the fear of God. When that is firmly established, all else can fall easily into place.

The scripture before us today resounds in a day when young men have polluted their lives with all manner of sin and evil. A quick perusal of the lives of Joseph and Daniel and one sees that the man who cleanses himself from earthly temptations opens the door for great blessing, promotions and favor. God was watching the lives of His servants and God is watching our lives today. God is always watching and those who labor to obey the Word of God, God labors to bless. The blessing when it comes will be overwhelming for we can never out-give God.

Becoming closely acquainted with the road map will be one of the greatest decisions you will ever make.

*Almighty God and King, thanks so much for the road map that YOU have provided for us. I take comfort in knowing that the wisdom, knowledge and understanding that I need is found in the pages of Your word. Let me be wise and humble enough to ask for directions from Your sourcebook so that I reach YOUR desired end for me.*

Month Four

The Believer's Manual

Week One

1. Where did Jesus say our true fulfillment in life comes from?

2. Explain why the Word of God is considered alive or living?

3. What is God speaking to you today? Make sure to take time not only to be communing with God but waiting or listening to what He has to say to you, determine now to do whatever He asks of you.

4. What is the last verse you memorized and pick a new verse from this last week?

## Day 98

## The Fire Is God

**"Is not My word like fire"—this is the Lord's declaration—"and like a hammer that pulverizes rock?** Jeremiah 23:29

Do you love jewellery? I tend to stay away from jewellery stores because I have very expensive taste. I own very little of the precious stuff, but I would love to spoil my wife with the finery that you can find only in a high-end jewellery store.

Gold comes in different carats and the process required to take gold from one level to another is more fire. The purification process is quite intense, but the results are remarkable. God declares in the scripture above that His Word is like fire. He is not speaking of a natural fire, but of a spiritual fire that burns up everything in our lives that holds us back from fulfilling His purpose and plans for us.

Fire is in a category all by itself. All life on earth fears fire. We recognize the all-consuming nature of fire and we do everything in our power to stop a fire before it starts. But not only does God declare that His Word is a fire, He Himself is declared as an "all-consuming fire"(Hebrews 12:29). This is not your typical description and yet we must come to grips with the nature and characteristics of fire that God also attributes to Himself. Scripture goes on to reveal that love, of which God is, is also declared to be like a fire in its protective nature towards anything that interrupt one's love affair (Hebrews 12:29; Song of Solomon 8:6). God declares Himself to be a jealous God and one that will wreak havoc on any who would try to turn our love from Him.

So when we consider that God is a consuming fire and His Word is a fire, we are brought to the realization that cleansing and purifying are a normal part of growing in God. God uses His Word and His presence to purge us and purify us. We do not conform to an outward set of rules that determine how we should live. No, instead the very nature and character of God is our standard and, by our intimate relationship with the Holy Spirit, we are empowered to do what God would do in any given situation.

It has been said for many years that only Christ can live the Christian life. He lives it through us as we are surrendered to Him and are obedient to the transformation process. I don't think like I use to think, speak like I use to speak or do what I used to do, all because of the new birth I experienced in Christ and my submission to follow God's way and not my way.

The Bible also says that God makes His servants a flame of fire (Hebrew 1:7). John Wesley, the great revivalist, was asked why thousands came to hear him preach. He said it was because he set himself on fire and people came to watch him burn. John Wesley's life was consumed with the love of God; he overflowed with evangelistic fervor and zeal for the lost.

When we become consumed with God's heartbeat, the fire on the inside begins to manifest on the outside. All will see our zeal and love for all that is God.

Am I a candidate? Are you?

*Daddy, we ask You to ignite our hearts afresh with love for Your deeper work in our lives that we might be transformed into Your image and likeness. Let our hearts burn with love for You and Your kingdom so that those who do not know You will be confronted with the reality of who You are and receive You into their hearts. You promised that You would baptize us with the Holy Spirit and with fire. Oh God send the fire we pray, Send the fire and purify us today.*

## Day 99

## The Rock Breaker

**"A hammer that breaks the rocks to pieces"** Jeremiah23:29

Today we look at the second half of the same verse, "My word is like a hammer that breaks the rocks to pieces."

Take a minute and read Jeremiah 29. I would encourage you to read it in the Message Bible if you have it available.

It does not take long to realize that God is really, really angry at the spiritual leaders who failed to minister to the people of God and to minister truth to the nation. Jeremiah 29 is a chapter in which God is angry at counterfeit leadership for giving false words from God, false dreams and false visions. God says "My Word, My Word when it is spoken brings incredible change, it burns and it destroys. You cannot hear a word from Me and not be affected."

Though God is fully capable of speaking a word of destruction over cities and nations, which is not His heart's desire. Jesus cursing the fig tree only proves how easily the world could be withered if He so choose.(Matthew 21:18-20) Instead God's hammer is used to destroy the strongholds and fortress built on the lies of hell in our lives. God's Word is a light that shines into the recess of our souls and shows us the lies holding us captive that we might be set free (Psalm 119:130). The strongholds and fortresses of many years can be disintegrated in seconds when we respond to the revelation of God's truths in our lives (2 Corinthians 10:4).

While in Uganda, my wife and I were discussing some negative aspects of my upbringing. I was taught a way of responding to racism that was detrimental to me and to those who were being racist. Though the intentions of my father were admirable, the methods were not God's. Angela said, "You did not have to be raised that way." That one sentence was used by God to enable me to release years of pain and frustration over issues that had never been in my control (how I was raised and how people treated me). What was in my control and is always in my control is how I choose to respond, no matter the issue. The hammer of truth obliterated any remaining vestiges of misunderstanding that held my past in pain. I could see so much clearer after the statement than I could before it was spoken.

God's Word is also a hammer to the enemy's plans and purposes when it is spoken in the mouth of one of his children in faith. The hammer of God's Word is greater than dynamite, nitroglycerin, nomadic drill or atomic bomb for that matter. No matter how great the lies of the enemy wrapped around a life, when faith is applied to the truth of God's Word, the enemy has to leave. When we fill our lives with the truth of God's Word, faulty thinking and ideas no longer have room in our lives because they no longer fit or make sense. For no other reason than that, we should be those who devour the Word of God on a constant basis. We should be those who invite the hammer of the Word to break of the lies and the deception that cling to us through our association with the world. Let us have a greater fervency and commitment to our love of God's Word.

*Daddy, hammer away. Break off the lies in my thinking that I am not even aware that I have. I want Your truth to be in the very core of my being. I want my thoughts to be centered on the truth of who You are and who I am in You.*

**Day 100**

**The Sword Of Heaven**

**"And the sword of the Spirit, which is the word of God;"** Eph. 6:17b

We have looked at the Word of God being a fire and a hammer. Today, we will look at how it is a sword.

The Apostle Paul was chained between two Roman guards in full battle array, which made it very easy for him to use their soldier's dress as the symbols of the Christians armor. Today, it would likely include a flak jacket, armor piercing bullets, and an M16 to put the enemy down. The point, of course, is for us to recognize that we are in a real fight against a real enemy that desires to destroy our lives and most definitely our testimony for Christ. There is no natural weapon available that we can use to defeat the hosts of darkness, but there are tried and true spiritual weapons at our disposal to enable us in putting the enemy to flight. We will look at more of these later in another series.

We have been enlisted, we are at war and our enemy takes no prisoners. He comes to steal, to kill and to destroy. To think that I can use weapons of natural mass destruction to defeat him is ludicrous. But what is not is learning from our Lord and Master Himself. The Word is a sword first and foremost only if you will believe it. In Jesus' conflict with the enemy, He used memorized scripture to defeat him at every turn. Satan could not withstand the power of God's Word rightly understood and applied.

When we believe God and take Him at His word we disarm Satan of his greatest tools of deception. The truth protects us from both lies and error, which quickly leads to outright deception. When we know the truth, it sets us free and enables us to live as God intended. Satan even used the Word of God with Jesus to try and ensnare Him. If he used it on Jesus, make no mistake he will use twisted scripture to try and deceive us or limit us at every turn.

No soldier goes to war without his gun. No policeman goes on duty without his firearm. Some actually bring extra weapons along just to be safe. When David went to battle against Saul, he was given "greater weapons" to use to enable him to defeat Goliath. David did not fight with them, however, because he had not "tested" them. This is an old way of saying that, not having used them before in a battle, he was uncertain of their ability. One thing is for sure, David knew his sling and he knew its ability. He was fully aware of how it would act in the day of battle.

The same must be said of any soldier's weapons. The same must also be said of our knowledge of God's Word. The more versed (no pun intended) in God's Word that we are, the more able we will be to put the enemy under our feet and keep him there. Do you want to overcome? Do you want to be victorious? How you treat the Word of God will determine the outcome of your life.

*King Jesus, thank You for Your living words and the power that is in them to transform a life and to defeat the enemy. As I read Your Word, I ask that You would highlight for me the truths I will need to win each battle that comes my way. Thank You for leading me into victory.*

## Day 101

### Victory through the Word

**"This is the victory that has conquered the world: our faith"** 1 John 5:4

**"The One who is in you is greater than the one who is in the world"** 1 John 4:4

Victory. This is not talking about a Super Bowl victory or of an Olympic gold medal, nor is it referring to victory over a literal enemy through armed combat. The greatest enemy in your life is someone you see every day. You interact with him as though you were the absolute best friends. Many times you take advice from your greatest enemy. You have grown to trust him and rely on him, and yet numerous times his answers have left you filled with pain and failure. You can find this enemy to your spiritual life in the mirror. Your greatest enemy is not the world, sin or the powers of darkness. The greatest enemy you will ever face is yourself. No person will let you down more than yourself.

Denying yourself and submitting to God and His way is the cornerstone to victory. How great to hear that greater is He that is IN YOU. Our key to victory is placed right down inside of us. As we are obedient to the Word of the Lord, we are assured of victory. As a matter of fact, the Word of God explains that God Himself will lead us into overwhelming triumph.

2 Corinthians 2:14a says, "Now thanks be to God who always leads us in triumph in Christ." The key here for us is that God is doing the leading and He will always lead us to triumph when we are in Christ. When we are outside of communion and obedience to Christ and the anointing, leading and guiding of the Holy Spirit, we get ourselves into trouble.

God led Israel into the Promised Land but the one time that they did not ask for God's help, they made a decision based on natural reasoning and were deceived. They ended up making a covenant with enemies that God had told them to destroy. Imagine making a covenant with your enemy to be their friend and to never harm them when God has told you to defeat them (Joshua 9). Had they inquired of God through the means that He had provided, the deception would have been uncovered. God's directions, as strange as they may seem to us, will always lead us to victory.

- Who ever heard of marching around a city seven times and shouting would bring victory? But it did (Joshua 6).
- When was the last time dipping yourself seven times in a dirty river would heal leprosy? But it did (2 Kings 5:14).
- When did washing spit out of your eyes in a specific pool heal blind eyes? But it did (John 9:1-7).

Have you ever seen iron float, time extended, a sea parted or dead people raised? All of these events and more happened through the direction of the Holy Spirit. When we obey, even when our sense and our senses tell us that something is impossible, that's God's territory. The impossible is possible with Him.

In a nutshell, obedience to the written Word and the spoken word of the Spirit will always end in personal victory and corporate triumph. Follow His leading and reap the benefits.

*I need victory in my life, Father, an overcoming life that You have provided by Christ's death and resurrection. I choose to live in obedience to Your Word and Your ways, even though I may not fully understand all that You may ask of me. I know You are faithful and I will see the victories in life that You have for me. I will help others walk into victory too.*

## Day 102

### Rightly Receiving the Word

**"And he said, Go, and tell this people, Hear ye indeed, but understand not; and see ye indeed, but perceive not. [10] Make the heart of this people fat, and make their ears heavy, and shut their eyes; lest they see with their eyes, and hear with their ears, and understand with their heart, and convert, and be healed."** Isaiah 6:9,10

These verses are quoted six times in the New Testament. That alone should cause us to stop, look and listen. When we consider that the statement, "The just shall live by faith" is in the New Testament three times and there are innumerable messages on those three major points, what attention and detail should we be giving to this heart-stopping message that God has repeated six times for us to hear!

Hear and understand what I am saying, God is calling for us to do, to really, really hear, but don't understand. He desires for us to see, really see, but because our hearts are not right toward him we are unable to incorporate the necessary change into your life. Our wickedness causes our heart to become fat, rich, gross and greasy. In other words, God is the God of your heart first and foremost. If your heart is right before God, His blessing will flow out to you and through you, even in the darkest, hardest seasons of your life. But if your heart is dark and prideful, selfish and self-centered, God will have nothing to do with you and you will forfeit the healing that your life so desperately needs.

Why do so many people miss out on the wonder and the glory of God that is made available to them? How do so called good, Christian, religious people miss out on the very fullness of who God is and what He desires to do in their lives?

The Apostle Paul met a man who had been used mightily by the enemy to deceive an entire region. When Paul came and brought healing and revelation to the region, the man appeared to have changed. But when people began to speak in tongues, this gentleman offered to purchase this power with money. His true heart was exposed and God brought discipline and judgment on him.

The famous story of Ananias and Sapphira also shows us that God always judges the heart, not just the deeds that we do.

In Jesus' ministry, the Pharisees gave gobs of money to receive the praise of men, but the widow gave all she had and so proved the true condition of her heart.

To hear what God has to say, to truly hear and understand and be continually converted and healed, your heart must be repentant, humble, broken and submitted. God and what He wants is all that matters. Culture, tradition, religion, family and self all lay down to God's will. When your heart is right before God, blessing, fruitfulness and His presence are a constant and the promise for healing can be realized. Let God recreate your heart and your whole world will be right. When your heart is right with God your entire life can be healed.

*"Create in me a clean heart O God and renew a right spirit within me" (Psalm 51:10).Pray through Psalm 51 today.*

## Day 103

## Continuing to Rightly Receive the Word

**``Therefore, ridding yourselves of all moral filth and evil, humbly receive the implanted word, which is able to save you``**. James 1:21

Today, we are going to continue looking at the condition of our hearts. God spoke through the prophet Isaiah and warned that if your heart is not right then you cannot receive the healing that God has for you. It does not matter how much you hear or even see of God's activities. Your *heart* determines how you will perceive and understand the works of God. Make it right and you will begin to automatically understand and incorporate God's will into your life.

We hear God's Word preached on a weekly basis and some people grow, some stagnate and some die spiritually. Why does one person arise and put into action the messages that they have heard while others do nothing with it and still others develop an attitude? Is there something wrong with the Word, something wrong with the church or something wrong with the Bible they are using?

Jesus said that those with a right heart can hear and see. If our hearts are not right, we cannot hear right and we cannot see right. What we hear will be twisted and turned into something other than what it was intended and we will look out and see a plan, an idea and a purpose other than what was meant.

Our hearts are always the issue. Cain had no reason to be jealous of his brother Abel. He had an equal opportunity to hear God's praise and acceptance. Instead, his jealous, bitter heart drove him to butcher his brother who had done him no wrong. Zacchaeus' heart was fully revealed when Jesus came over to his house. He declared publicly, "If I have wronged you, I will repay four times what I took from you." Jesus said, "Salvation has come to this house today" (Luke 19:1-4).

A right heart enables us to application

l down the lies that we have believed about God, ourselves and others. We can than live out of a place of gratitude, compassion and sincerity instead of ingratitude, selfishness and lack of integrity.

To hear God, to see His Kingdom come and to be a part of making it happen necessitates that we first have a heart that is God-centered, then others-centered and then, lastly, focused on self. Everything that Jesus did was for His Father's glory; He was absolutely selfless and focused on lifting up His Father's name. If we want to hear right so that we can think right so that we can live right, then first and foremost we must get our hearts right. We need to be transparent with God and humble so that we are pliable in God's hands. We need to be teachable to learn how to respond to what God puts in front of us. The more we respond to the conviction the Holy Spirit brings to our lives, the more He will entrust to us as we are obedient to what He asks.

*Sadly, Father, there are servants of Yours who have gone astray. I am learning there was something in their heart that was not submitted and given over to You. I give You my heart again and again and again. Have your way so that I can live Your way for your glory. "Search me Oh God, and know my heart; test me and know my concerns. See if there is see any offensive/wicked way in me; lead me in the everlasting way" (Psalm 139:23-24).*

## Day 104

### Ingesting the Word

**"So I went to the angel and asked him to give me the little scroll. He said to me, "Take and eat it; it will be bitter in your stomach, but it will be as sweet as honey in your mouth." Then I took the little scroll from the angel's hand and ate it. It was as sweet as honey in my mouth, but when I ate it, my stomach became bitter. And I was told, "You must prophesy again about many peoples, nations, languages, and kings."** Revelation 10:9-11

Ingesting God's Word and digesting God's Word are two different things. We can ingest the Word of God through reading, through sermons and even through memorization. These processes, as well as many others, enable God's Word to come into our lives. But just because it comes *into* our lives does not mean that it will come *out of* our lives. In other words, what comes out of you when the going gets tough? Do God's principles of life come out of you or is it a reaction of your soul and your flesh?

God has always desired that we incarnate His Word, like the little boy who, after a discipline, weeping when told to take it to God in prayer, replied, "I need a Jesus with skin on". He needed a physical representation of God. A hug, a kiss, a word of encouragement—not a room filled with directions or words of comfort. It is not that God can't provide those things in a very real way, but He intended us to be His hands showing His heart in action.

We should not be surprised that Jesus says healing will flow through our hands. It is as we actually touch the infirmed with love that healing takes place. Like Jesus, we need to touch the lepers of our day, breaking the spirit of rejection off of their lives. That is ingesting the Word, taking it from the unseen to the seen. Putting flesh on the truth, living it out in such a way that both the world and the church can see that our lives are directed by the principles of God's Word.

We all like the honey part of the word of God, but we are not big on the bitter part. In God's economy you cannot have one without the other. Having a prophetic word given to you is "sweet", but living in such a way to bring it to pass will require going through some bitter storms in life.

Psalm 105 tells us in short-form the story of Joseph. Joseph received a prophetic dream in his youth but it took a life time to fulfill. Before the fulfillment started to take place, Joseph was sold as a slave and then found himself in prison for a crime he did not commit. God's Word says that His Promise/His Word/His destiny was testing Joseph to see what he was made of. Was he made of the stuff that could handle the fulfilled dream and promise? A certain level of character had to be in place for Joseph to ascend to be the second most powerful man on the planet. When God's work was completed, the bitterness had turned sweet again because of Joseph's character. In one day, a prisoner was turned into a Prime Minister. Joseph had seen the one who is invisible and began to mirror Him. He was living a lifestyle that ingested the Word.

*Father I thank You that You still turn prisoners into Prime Ministers. Help me, in each stage of my life, to always put my trust in Your unfailing ability to turn any circumstance around for Your glory. I don't want to be a hearer of the Word only, I want to be a doer, one who lives out what Your Holy Spirit is teaching me.*

## Day 105

### Meditating on the Word

**How happy is the man who does not follow the advice of the wicked or take the path of sinners or join a group of mockers! Instead, his delight is in the Lord's instruction, and he meditates on it day and night. He is like a tree planted beside streams of water that bears its fruit in season and whose leaf does not wither. Whatever he does prospers.** Psalm 1:1-3

One of the great definitions of meditating is to "chew it like cud", which is an allusion to what a cow does with its food. Apparently they have more than one stomach and will regurgitate food to get all of the nutrients out of it before the stomach will process the food.

God tells us that He has secrets in His Word waiting for us to dig out. It is the glory of God to conceal a matter, but it is the glory of kings to search it out (Proverbs 25:2). God's thoughts are not our thoughts and God's ways are not our ways (Isaiah 55:8-9). When we truly believe this, it will motivate us to meditate more and more on His precious Word.

David said in Psalm 119:99, "I have more insight than all my teachers because Your decrees are my meditation." Other translations use the word "wiser than" to convey what meditating on God's Word will do for any individual. We are called to train our minds in the process of researching the truths hidden in the Word of God. As God highlights a verse of scripture in your life, in your devotions or through a message, the Spirit of God is calling you to digging deeper so that the truth of His Word to you becomes meat to your spirit and food for those around you. As you meditate on a scripture from God, you are making it clear to God you desire Him to talk to you and unveil His Word to your mind. You will be amazed at how quickly scriptural truths, gems, doctrine, wisdom and understanding will be given to you without even asking because you fill your mind with the truth of God's Word.

Meditating, as some of us know it, is based on the spiritual component primarily in yoga or eastern mysticism where one is encouraged to "empty one's mind". Here, the complete opposite is true. We fill our minds instead with specific scriptures so that insight, illumination, revelations, wisdom, knowledge and understanding can be given to us while we meditate on the truth of God's Word.

Ever had a math problem in school or a riddle that someone gave you that was impossible to solve? Some people just give up and decide it is too hard for them. Others jump in with both feet and start the process of figuring it out. They are determined to find the answer so they will ask questions, read books, ask their parents (WOW), etc. If only we would approach the Word of God the same way when we have a question or have a need! If only we would be like Jacob and the Shunammite woman – both of them held onto the representatives of God until they got the blessing they were in need of.(Genesis 32:24-31,2 Kings 4:18-37) Minds like that will always find the answer, get the blessing, increase in anointing and prosper in all things. Meditating is a way of life that calls all believers into a lifestyle of not just reading the Word of God, but loving the Author so much that they ponder His words until the fullness of His intent is realized in their lives.

The choice is yours.

Precious Holy Spirit YOU are invited here in my life and in my meditations, would YOU direct my heart and my thoughts to the truths YOU know I need to fulfill YOUR will and plan for my life. As I meditate on YOUR Word, illuminate YOUR truths to my life. Thank YOU that this is YOUR joy and desire to make YOUR truths known to my life.

Week Two

1. In your own words explain the statement 'only Christ can live the Christian life"? What relevance does that have on our day to day living?

2. What happens to the lies of the enemy when faith is applied to the truth of God's word?

3. When our heart is right with God what will happen to our whole life?

4. A right heart enables us to tear down what three lies?

5. What is the difference between ingesting the Word of God and digesting the Word of God?

6. Quote last week's verse and pick a new one.

## Day 106

### Memorize the Word

But He answered, **"It is written;** Matthew 4:4

Jesus told him, **"It is also written**; Matthew 4:7

Then Jesus told him, **"Go away, Satan! For it is written:** Matthew 4:10

The highest call on the life of every believer is to be like Jesus. The highest compliment paid to the disciples in Antioch in Acts 11 is that they were called Christians or "little Christ's". Though the people meant it as a rebuke, it was indeed the highest praise possible. I am sure if we were physically present in the same room and I asked you if you wanted to be like Jesus, you would immediately indicate to me that it is indeed your heart's cry.

There are myriads of character qualities and perfect, sinless examples from Christ that one could begin to teach on, but the one that I want to take a minute and examine this day is the memorization of God's Word. When Jesus was twelve years old and in the temple, He was already a student of the Word of God. Most likely, like the Pharisees with whom He was talking, He had already memorized the Pentateuch (the first five books of the Bible).

When Jesus was confronted with a head on, no holds barred, UFC, MMA, boxing extravaganza, He did not hold back any punches. He fought the adversary mano-a-mano and His weapon of choice against the trickery of hell was the memorized Word, the sword of the Spirit, the never-changing Word of God. All three of the quotes that Jesus addressed Satan with came from the fifth Book of the Pentateuch – the book of Deuteronomy – the Book of Remembrance or of the Second reading. Satan had no defence, not because it was Jesus He was fighting but because the truth of God's Word applies to everybody in every situation. Satan's most hideous weapon that he has against you and me is deception. When we believe a lie and doubt God's Word, Satan becomes both the accuser and the tormentor in that area of our lives. He will build a stronghold there to hinder us.

The lesson to be learned is to know God's Word, to memorize it just like Jesus did. He did not draw on His Godhood to defeat Satan, He showed mankind the purest, most effective, fastest most assured way of all: feed Satan the truth, make him swallow his lies and let him know that, as for us, we will take God at His Word and not allow lies and deception to turn us from the light into the darkness.

As you and I seek God through His Word, certain scriptures at certain seasons are going to be extremely meaningful and inspiring. These are verses that are going to enable us to bear fruit in our lives as we take heed to the words and apply them.

*To know You more, Lord, is within my grasp if I will discipline myself and memorize Your Word. I know it is a choice and I choose to approach Your word with hunger and desire, to seek Your truth that I might be set free from lies that hinder me. I choose to memorize Your Word, to hide it in my heart that I might not sin against You. I choose to make it my daily bread, that like Israel in the wilderness, I will eat the heavenly manna that is prepared for me.*

## Day 107

## Read the Word

**I have treasured Your word in my heart so that I may not sin against You.** Psalm 119:1

**Let the word of Christ dwell in you richly in all wisdom, teaching and admonishing one another in psalms and hymns and spiritual songs, singing with grace in your hearts to the Lord.** Colossians 3:16

There are a lot of bestsellers out there today raking in the millions and winning numerous awards. I will even go as far and say they are transforming lives, transforming them but usually not in the right direction. We live in a day now with portable e-readers making it possible for people to access newspapers, magazines, periodicals enabling people to reading everywhere. But what in fact are they reading about? Interesting thing to consider, God wrote a book. He actually took the time to write a book for us in order to convey His heart, mind, plans and purposes. The most amazing aspect of it though is that it is a love story. A story of love known, love forsaken and love bought back at the highest possible price. God wrote a book; it is the best seller to this very day.

Though I desire to go into the history of how the Word of God was written down and the price that was paid by servants of God to enable us to have it in print, I will forbear. But let me quickly say, not only was your salvation purchased with blood, but God's Word came to you by the ultimate sacrifices paid by numerous servants of God down through the ages, martyred to ensure that you and I would have the Word of God in our own language, easily accessible for all of us.

Communicating to His people is of the utmost significance to God. He longs for people to hear and know who He is and what He desires. God gave us His Word, but the question is what time and attention do we give to it? Reading it, is just the starting point. It is pointless to hear what God says and then not do it. We need to hear and obey.

No parent would ever be satisfied with a child who could reiterate every word they spoke but never did anything they asked. As a parent, the purpose of my speaking is not just communion and relationship, but obedience. When I ask my child to do something, I expect that they will do what I have asked. We all remember the times we tell our parents, "I never heard you."

Well God made it simple. It's in the book. So we don't read the book and we think that lets us off the hook. Too late, our conscience has been redeemed and knows right from wrong. Now it comes down to obeying what He is speaking. Reading the Word keeps us in constant communion with the Lord, helps us keep our minds on Him and enables us to have a ready word for those in need around us. God never fails to fill us with His revelation and understanding of who He is if we will just cling to the revelation He has given us through His Word.

If you do not have a plan to read through the Word of God, there are numerous ones available to you. The simplest way to read through the Bible from cover to cover in one year is to simply read three chapters a day. Start in the New Testament and then go to the Old Testament. We want to focus on Jesus and who He is to us. We find Him through types and shadows revealed throughout the Old Testament. Make the choice to set aside time every day to be in the Word of God that the Word of God might be in you and available through you to others.

*Pray as you feel led.*

## Day 108

## Speak the Word

**But what does it say? "The word is near you, in your mouth and in your heart" that is, the word of faith which we preach.**" Romans 10:8 New King James

Over the last couple of days, a pattern has been emerging as to how the Word of God encompasses our entire lives—what we think, what we meditate on, how we do warfare, what we ingest into our lives and how we actually live our lives. All of these things are centered on the Word of God. It is not by mistake that God proclaimed that man would not live by bread, but by every word that would proceed from the mouth of God (Deuteronomy 8:3).

One area of our lives that we have touched on so far has the greatest significance. The reason I say that is because the Word teaches us that "life and death are in the power of the tongue" (Proverbs 18:21) and it takes a perfect man to be able to bridle/control his tongue (James 3). When we look at the life of Jesus, the incarnate Word, what transfixed the people by His ministry was two things: a) He taught with authority, and b) He demonstrated that authority by healing and delivering people from the powers of sin, sickness, disease and death.

Jesus' words lined up with who He was on the inside. What came out of His lips was perfectly in alignment with what was on the inside of His spirit and soul. There was a perfect unity. There was no discord and no disagreement. Perfect unity unlocked heaven's power and will into the earth.

When we ask God for many righteous, holy and pure requests that line up with the will of God but there is disunity in us—whether it is a lack of faith, hypocrisy, unresolved sin or doubt—God cannot answer. Samson is the greatest figure that would seem to function with impunity, great sin in his life and great power working simultaneously. But although God fulfilled His covenant promise to Samson, there was a leanness that went into his soul that became evident when he broke his covenant with God. Only when he was in unity in his spirit, his soul and his body could God answer his prayer again. He restored his covenant with God; his soul was no longer under conviction for gross hypocrisy and sin; and his hair had grown back. All three were in place when God answered his last prayer perfectly (Judges 15, 16).

When our spirit, soul and body are in agreement, functioning in faith and in purity, God is free to move. One aspect of our soul being in alignment is that our mind, will and emotions all say the same thing in true faith. We are in agreement with the Word of God from the inside out. We speak the Word out of our spirit. Our emotions are not in conflict but in agreement, showing excited faith and expecting God's answer. Our will opens our mouth to bring forth declarations of faith in God of what we believe He will do in our lives. Our words turn the tides of nations by what we believe and what we declare.

The more we speak the negative over our lives it becomes a self-fulfilling prophesy. You cannot speak poverty, sickness, despair, depression and end up with riches, health, joy and contentment. It simply does not work that way. But when we see who we are in Christ, not what our circumstances are or how we feel, then we have the opportunity to function in life from our position in Christ, seated in the heavenly places. I’ve got a funny feeling that if we try it, we just might like it. Let the words of our mouths declare our innermost heart's desire, releasing the power of the Holy Spirit to work miraculously to build His church in us.

*Daddy, my hearts cry is to live speaking Your truths to every element of my life and world. Let boldness be my portion as I fill my heart with who You are. Let a heart of faith produce a mouth of faith and declarations of faith that will see Your glory and power displayed in the earth and through my life.*

## Day 109

## Live the Word

**"Therefore, everyone who hears these words of Mine and acts on them will be like a sensible man who built his house on the rock. [25] The rain fell, the rivers rose, and the winds blew and pounded that house. Yet it didn't collapse, because its foundation was on the rock. [26] But everyone who hears these words of Mine and doesn't act on them will be like a foolish man who built his house on the sand. [27] The rain fell, the rivers rose, the winds blew and pounded that house, and it collapsed. And its collapse was great!"** Matthew 7:24-27

While living in Uganda, we had a torrential storm one night. It was the closest thing to hurricane force winds that I had ever experienced. We lived in a house that was very well constructed so we had no damage to our home, but those who lived in very poor conditions were devastated by the storm. Those whose homes that were made of a mixture of mud and cement lost not only their homes, but some lost their lives.

The news informs us of times in developing countries when storms come and lives are lost. Jesus uses this illustration to show us that this is the inevitable result of living by our own means, of doing it our way and not God's way. Jesus was giving a real world definition of what happens when we do not obey His Word. When we obey God's Word, the assured result will be blessing, stability, longevity and prosperity in more than just the financial realm.

The worst and greatest form of pride is spiritual pride, which goes hand in hand with deception. Pride centered on spiritual activity is wretched and I am guilty of it. The Pharisees were guilty of spiritual pride as well. Saul, who later turned to Paul, was guilty of spiritual pride and he found himself responsible for the deaths of numerous Christians. So in the midst of talking about not hearing God's Word in vain and living out what we are commanded, I want to make it clear it is not what we do that is the key focus because we are not saved by works. Who we are is the ultimate issue. We should show mercy because we are merciful; we should forgive because we have been forgiven; we are compassionate and loving because of Christ in us; we serve because we have a servant's heart and not because it gets us points with the Pastor. Doing never comes before being and that is the wonderful truth of the Christian experience.

Jesus' parable of the Pharisee and the sinner enables us to see whether we are living in humility or in pride (Luke 18:9-14). The focus should not be on us and what we have done. No, the focus belongs on Him and on what He has done and is doing. Grace has enabled you; grace has saved you; grace has led you. To Him and Him alone be the glory for all that He has done in us and through us.

The wonder and excitement of being in right standing with God is that when we look into His Word and see His activity and holy working, we realize that He desires to do the exact same in us and through us.

Yeah God, Praises to Your Name, how boring would it be to see the wondrous events of Your word and to believe that there are none available for today. How exhilarating to know that every day I can be an instrument in YOUR hand as I obey YOUR word and live by its principles. I not only store up treasure in heaven but I bring change to the world I live in….

## Day 110

### Interpreting the Scriptures

**``Then beginning with Moses and all the Prophets, He interpreted for them the things concerning Himself in all the Scriptures.``** Luke 24:27

The disciples had the privilege of being with Jesus for three and a half years. During that time, they heard the teachings of Jesus and saw how He handled the scriptures, interpreting them so they could understand what He was talking about. But you will find that they had a limited grasp on what Jesus communicated openly. Many times they came to Him and said, "What are You talking about? We don't understand. Explain it to us, please?" Every time Jesus spoke of His upcoming death and resurrection, for example, they totally missed it. Yet, it was clearly "revealed" in the Old Testament that this would take place. (Easy for us to say 2000 years after the fact. They were living it.)

After Jesus went to the cross and died for their sins, the disciples were in hiding, fearing for their very lives. Along came Jesus on the road to Emmaus, appearing to two of the disciples. He joined their conversation and, soon enough, began to "explain thoroughly and to interpret" for them what the Old Testament had to say about Him being the Messiah/the Christ (Luke 24:27). Imagine Jesus showing them:

- I am the Seed of Eve sent to crush the serpent's head (Genesis 3:15).
- I am the Ark of Noah where all find refuge from the flood (Genesis 9).
- I am the Coat of Many Colors revealing the Father's love and many-faceted grace of God upon the races (Genesis 37:3).
- I am the true Seed of Abraham, the true Isaac (laughter) of the Father's heart (Genesis 22).
- I am Jacob's Wrestler (Genesis 32:24 - 32).
- I am Joseph's Wisdom.(Genesis 41:16)
- I am the fulfillment of Joseph, rejected by his brethren, overcomer of temptation, imprisoned though guiltless, punished yet victorious, risen to the highest seat next in power to only one other. (Philippians 2:5-11)

And we are not even close to exhausting what is in Genesis, never mind the rest of the Old Testament. The disciples would have been stupefied as He rhymed His way from Genesis to Malachi. No wonder they said that their hearts burned within them as He explained the scriptures to them.

Are you ready for seasons of "heartburn", times in which God opens the scriptures to you so that you might see who He truly is or what He is doing in the earth? Please note that, for all intents and purposes, the disciples had not even asked God to thoroughly explain it to them. Yet God, out of love for them and the desire for them to be mature, stepped down yet again and revealed truth.

*God open my understanding. Open my heart to understand and to see You in scriptures and in life where I would miss You. As I read Your Word, give me understanding and revelation that I might understand and apply what is before me. I know that there are mysteries and wonders awaiting me in Your Word. Help me not to walk in pride, for knowledge leads to pride. Instead, let me humbly acknowledge that You enable me to know Your ways so that I can teach others.*

## Day 111

## Applying the Revelation

**"Then He opened their minds to understand the Scriptures"** Luke 24:45

You can imagine the joy and excitement in the hearts of the two disciples that leapt up from their table and ran back to Jerusalem so that they could confirm to the rest of the disciples that Jesus was indeed raised from the dead. But just as they related their story to them, Jesus appeared to all of them. They are stupefied and terrified as Jesus proceeds to let them touch Him and watch Him eat so they can see that He is physical and not metaphysical or spirit.

Now that the disciples accepted that Jesus was actually standing in front of them in the flesh and it was not a vision, their physical senses were not lying to them, Jesus lets them know that another step is necessary for them to move on in God. They had a revelation of the Risen Christ but not all those who did lived it out. There were over five hundred people who saw the resurrected Christ at one time, but only one hundred and twenty were in the upper room praying for the promise of the Father. What happened to the three hundred and eighty people? (1 Corinthians 15:6; Acts 1:15)It is one thing to properly interpret the scriptures and to put all the pieces together, but it is another thing altogether to comprehend it and apply it to your life.

The application of God's Word to our lives is paramount. 1 Corinthians 8:1 tells us that knowledge can lead to pride, so the more knowledgeable we become in anything, the greater the opportunity for pride. It is so easy for pride to sneak in and influence our hearts to think more of ourselves than we should. How do we guard against pride, live the word? In attempting to live the word in our own strength, we immediately find that we simply cannot do it. Only Christ can live the Christian life, so we must submit ourselves to the dealings of God which will effectively do away with our pride. We need to submit ourselves in humility and dependence on God realizing that what we know and understand is not nearly as important as what we are actually living.

Application of truth outweighs knowledge of truth any day. We cannot make an idol out of scriptural revelation or understanding, although this is easy to do in an academic society where we are taught that education is the savior of mankind. The application of truth is where God awaits us to move in might and in power. When God's people have a mental assent to scriptural truth than God is unable to do wonders and work miracles for a mental assent to God's power and willingness are not enough. But when we move to a place of knowing that right here and right now God will perform wonders because we ask than we are living in a place where God will do wonders on our behalf. We live in the reality that Jesus is the same yesterday, today and forever and He will not fail us.

- Peter got out of the boat and walked on water, because initially, he believed. (Matthew 14:29)

- Gideon took God at His word and routed the Midianites, because Gideon came to a place of trusting God. (Judges 6 -8 )

- Peter let down his net at Christ's command and received a boat load of fish. It only happened because Peter took Him at His word. (Luke 5:1-6)

- David ran to meet Goliath anticipating the victory, know that only faith can motivate that kind of response. (1 Samuel 17:48)

- Elijah actually showed up on Mt. Carmel to face 850 prophets of Baal, because he knew God as God.( 1 Kings 18)

- Remember that only the person who brings an umbrella to a prayer meeting for rain actually has faith.

It is more than getting revelation from God or fully comprehending its significance. What it actually comes down to is how we are going to live it out. Being moulded into Christ's image is the desire of every believer, and this process is only brought to completion because we conform our lives to His image by our obedience and submission to His will (Philippians 2:12).

Yes to Your ways Lord and Yes to Your will in my life. Thank –You for the opportunity I have every day to put into the practice the truths You are teaching me. I may not do it perfectly every day and some days I may miss it altogether but I have another opportunity the next day and You will never abandon me and will always be there to enable me. My hope is fixed on You and on Your promises and with great expectation I go in to today to put into practice what I am learning….

**Day 112**

**Deliverance through the Word**

**For though we live in the body, we do not wage war in an unspiritual way[1] [4] since the weapons of our warfare are not worldly but are powerful through God for the demolition of strongholds. We demolish arguments [5] and every high-minded thing that is raised up against the knowledge of God, taking every thought captive to obey Christ.**2 Corinthians 10:3.4

In our journey of life, we quickly come to an understanding that we are not alone. We recognize that God is real and, therefore, the spiritual realm is real and is the originator of all things natural and spiritual. Life is first and foremost spiritual and then it is natural.

Sin has helped to switch the order so that we see things naturally first and spiritually last. Our enemy, our adversary, the devil, more accurately called Satan, is like a roaring lion, seeking who he may devour. Give him the opportunity and he will gum you to death. It is no wonder that the Apostle Paul warned us, "Give no place to the devil" (Ephesians 4:27). The word "place" is a word which refers to a specific location, as opposed to a spacious public place like a park or a circus. It refers to a more personal spot: my life, my house, my family. Paul warns us not to give Satan any access for he will take it and use it against you.

Our battle is spiritual and so it requires spiritual weapons. The primary offensive weapon we have is the sword of the spirit, which is the Word of God. We have examined this earlier in this section. We saw how King Jesus used the sword of the Word to defeat the lies of the enemy. We are all susceptible to Satan's deceptive lies, used specifically to cause us to doubt God's Word and His promises to us. Adam and Eve are the perfect example of this and how the Word of God was twisted to cause them to doubt God and walk into sin and rebellion.

The Bible tells us to not be ignorant of Satan's devices; he uses the same tools for one reason alone and that is because they keep working. But we are commanded to demolish his strongholds, his arguments and any high-minded reasoning that would tear us from the truth in Christ. Any elevated attitude that would make us doubt God's Word and live our way instead of His way is from the enemy. The Apostle John, called it "the spirit of antichrist" and he was 100% correct. (I John 4:3)

Jesus said that we would know the truth and the truth would set us free (John 8:32). Our hunger precedes our freedom. Those willing to stay in bondage will stay oppressed, depressed and even possessed. But the one who demands freedom need only call on the name of the Lord and proclaim the truth of God's will over their situation. Freedom from Satan's snares is a normal, ongoing process of spiritual growth. The lies of the enemy that we believe are what hold us back from experiencing all that God has for us. When the lie is broken, freedom comes and the liberty to enjoy life is regained.

As long as we believe that we were meant to be ruled over as slaves, we will continue to live such an existence. But when we realize that we were created to rule and reign with God, we will not settle to be captive to anything, particularly to any sin in our lives. We will zealously seek to walk in the full freedom that Christ purchased for us when He died on the cross. Satan's lies will have no more place in our lives.

*Thank You for the freedom to live in victory. It is for freedom that You have set us free. You have declared that fear has torment and no Father would stand for their child to be in torment. Your perfect love casts out fear and any other restraint or darkness in my life.*

## Day 113

### Revelation from the Word

**But now, brothers, if I come to you speaking in other languages, how will I benefit you unless I speak to you with a revelation or knowledge or prophecy or teaching?** 1 Corinthians 14:6

In 1 Corinthians 14:6, the Apostle Paul is writing to the church, giving wisdom and direction to them as how to be the Church of Jesus Christ. Paul explains that in the church meeting, everything must result in edification. He fully believed in and practiced the proliferation of the gifts of the Holy Spirit, but with this understanding: "Let all that is to be done be done for mutual profit, done decently and be done in order." Paul communicates some different ways in which messages are given both to the minister and to the believer and they are by revelation, by knowledge (study), by prophesying and by teaching. Today, we want to focus on how God ministers to you through revelation from His Word.

As you spend time in the word of God, He is going to give you revelation—a disclosure of truth concerning things before unknown. When God opened my eyes to who He is and how much He loved me, I became immediately addicted to His Word. Nobody told me to read His Word, but it became the most important book in my life. I read it and memorized it and shared it and sang it and prayed it and cried it. In the process of loving God's Word and hungering after His Word, revelation after revelation of truth began being downloaded into my heart and mind. I knew truths that I didn't even know I knew about God's Word and nature because of my time in His Word. To my great heart's delight, God opened the door to Bible School and I basked in the joy of being able to study God's Word full time, seeing how much I did not know and being given the privilege of being able to learn more. (Just a little side note: Since the scriptures are a revelation of a Person whom we will spend eternity getting to know, no one can ever exhaust the wonder and the awe of discovery as we unlock more of who God is through the scriptures.) It is the hungry heart that will be fed and given riches beyond our wildest imaginations.

If I were sitting in front of you, you would see tears in my eyes and a glow on my face coming from deep within my heart and spirit. You would see in me a passion and a hunger for loving the Word of God because it is a tool and an instrument that God has ordained to reveal Himself and to be the measuring stick of truth for all doctrine and understanding. Eat the book! Eat the book! Eat the book! God is on the other side beckoning you into Himself, into His glory and into revelations of who He was and is and ever will be. He is calling you to Himself that He might love you and bless you, anoint you and fill you with joy unspeakable and full of glory.

*Yes Lord. Yes Lord. More of You Lord. More of You. I want More of You.*

## Week Three

1. What will obedience to God's written word and His indwelt voice always result in?

2. The application of truth outweighs…….?

3. What is the worst form of pride and what goes hand in hand with it?

4. What happens to us when we come to the realization that God created us to rule and reign the universe with Him?

5. Quote last week's verse and pick a new one.

## Day 114

### Ears to Hear - Obey The Word

**Jesus answered, The first and principal one of all commands is: Hear, O Israel, The Lord our God is one Lord; And you shall love the Lord your God out of and with your whole heart and out of and with all your soul your life and out of and with all your mind with your faculty of thought and your moral understanding and out of and with all your strength. This is the first and principal commandment. The second is like it and is this; You shall love your neighbor as yourself. There is no other commandment greater than these.** Mark 12:29-31 Amplified

I would like to continue on the topic that I started yesterday. It goes without saying that God is a communicator. He is always communicating to us. Do we recognize that sometimes we have ears to hear and sometimes we do not have ears to hear? It is not a coincidence that Jesus said many times at the end of parables or teachings, "He who has ears let him hear." And then, in the book of Revelation, we also have the statement being made, "He who has ears let him hear what the Spirit is saying to the church." These statements in and of themselves teach us very clearly that we can pray, read spiritual material, be in church and seek God and yet still not hear exactly what He's trying to communicate to us.

I've always found it interesting that when the lawyers came to Jesus and asked Him what the greatest commandment is, He broke it down into a three part answer. In the clearest of terms, Jesus felt that it was impossible to have just one answer to the question of what is the greatest command of all. His response if he was a teacher in a university or in a classroom might have been a little bit like this:

1) People of God **listen, listen, listen** to what God has to say. It is your primary responsibility to hear and to obey what God says.
2) The number one command that God gives to you is that you are to love him.
3) The evidence that you are obeying the first command is that you love others as you love yourself.

When you are seeking God and He answers you, His answers are going to fall into one of these three areas. He will enable you to be a greater servant, a greater lover of God and a greater lover of others.

We get ourselves into trouble like Jonah when we run out on God because we think we know better what God should do in a situation or circumstance. Been there, done that, got the certificate and the trophy and felt so empty. Our hearing is vital to our being able to fulfill God's will in our lives, not in what we do, but in who He has called us to BE.

*Daddy, I lived for so long not ever hearing Your voice or knowing Your will, now I am able to live in both. I am so thrilled in my heart and mind. Let me never take for granted what Jesus did so that I could hear Your voice and respond in righteousness. Give me ears to hear. That is what I am praying for. Give us ears to hear what Your Spirit is saying and a heart to obey. Yes Lord, a heart to obey.*

## Day 115

## Anointing Through the Word

**"And unleaveded bread, unleavened cakes mixed with oil, and unleavened wafers anointed with oil you shall make them of wheat flour."** Exodus 29:2

**"Then Jacob rose early in the morning, and took the stone that he had put at his head, set it up as a pillar, and poured oil on top of it"** Genesis 18:18

Jesus, the perfect Son of God, laid aside His divinity and became the prototypical man. He showed us how all of us should live our lives. It is not a coincidence that His ministry did not begin until He was baptized in water and in the Spirit. From that day on, He was identified not simply as Jesus of Nazareth, nor as Jesus son of Mary and Joseph, but as Jesus the Christ. The Christos speaks of the anointed one, the one on whom the Holy Spirit dwells without measure. The divine collaboration between Jesus the Son of God and the Person of the Holy Spirit enabled Jesus to perform the great signs and wonders that accompanied His ministry.

Throughout the Bible, the anointing is what made the difference for great kings, prophets, queens, priests and judges. All sought a greater diffusion of the Holy Spirit's personhood and power. The Holy Spirit who penned the Word is also the greatest interpreter of the Word. The Holy Spirit who performed the miracles of the Word is also the only conduit of the power in the Word.

We are helpless without the work of the Holy Spirit. The Holy Spirit's anointing gives us the knowledge and the wherewithal to accomplish the will of God in every situation. The greater the infilling/overflowing of the Holy Spirit we are, the more capable we are of fulfilling God's mission and purposes in the earth. The Word of God and our obedience to Him enriches the anointing of God in our lives and positions us for greater usefulness in His kingdom.

God worked with the apostles, confirming their words with signs and wonders. God does not change. He desires to the same today. Though the anointing is a Person, the Spirit and the Word are forever in agreement. The greater revelation and illumination we have from the Word of God by the Spirit , the more the Holy Spirit will work and move through us to glorify Christ and reveal Him to the lost and dying. We see in the scriptures before us today the prophetic shadow of the Bread of Life being anointed with the Holy Spirit. If Jesus did not function without the Holy Spirit, how much more should our dependence and cry for the Holy Spirit be evident in our lives?

Holy Spirit, You are welcome here. I need more of You and ask that You would overflow me. I know I can do nothing without You, as you fill me to overflowing I will be an instrument in Your hand for Your glory.

## Day 116

### Healing In the Word

**"He forgives all your sins, He heals all your diseases."** Psalm 103:3

The Bible is a supernatural book which begins with the supernatural creation of the universe under the hand of Almighty God. The bible begins with the words, "In the Beginning, God…" (Genesis 1:1) If you can't conceive of believe the first four words of the first book of the Bible, than you are going to have a huge problem with the rest of the books. If we come to the Bible the same way as we come to any other book, even books about the Bible, than we are cutting ourselves off from all that God has for us. God, who is omnipotent, who made the heavens and the earth, is unlimited in power still reveals Himself through works of power and might.

I could share with you a number of times in my personal life where I have seen the miraculous intervention of god in healing – in the very simplest of miracles, where you might say, "oh you just got better" to recognizing without a doubt that God divinely intervened and He alone can get the flory and praise for wheat he has done. Jesus told us to believe that He is who He said that He was and as the Son of God, risen from the dead and ascended on high, He gave gifts to men and one of those gifts is the "gifts of healing" (1 Corinthians 12:9) You may be someone who has that gift. He is the same person who said to us that signs and wonders would follow the life of a believer and that we would lay hands on the sick and they MIGHT recover, or they SHOULD recover. Or did he mean that as we use medicine and prayer that they would recover. That is not what He said, He said that we would pray and we would put our hands on people and THEY WOULD BE HEALED.

The Bible, both Old and New Testaments, is filled with the miraculous intervention of God through healing. Sickness and death are a result of sin. When god made us, He did not make us to be sick and die. He hates disease, sickness and death and desires that we be whole and healthy, as any parent would desire for their children. As you read the Word of God and come to testimonies too good to be true, stop right there and declare, "If God is not too good to be true, then His wonders and His works are not to good to be true."

If you knew somebody who was given an inheritance that was worth millions of dollars and yet they refused to inquire to see whether or not the lawyers were telling the truth, what would you think of such a person? We would all agree there is something wrong with them. It is no different for you and me when it comes to the miraculous intervention of god. All the signs and wonders in the Bible up until the cross of Christ occurred under the Old Covenant mandate, but after the cross, with the New Covenant instituted by His blood, death and resurrection, there are greater promises, greater anointing, greater power and therefore greater expectations. The blood of Jesus has prevailed for us. He died and rose. The inheritance has been activated. The down payment is the Holy Spirit, so the rest is glory indeed.

*I come expectant, Daddy, to Your mighty Word. Let my soul boast in who You are and what You desire to do. I pray that faith would captivate my heart as I read Your Word to believe for Your greatness to be seen in me.*

## Day 117

## Share the Word

**This book of instruction must not depart from your mouth; you are to recite it day and night so that you may carefully observe everything written in it. For then you will prosper and succeed in whatever you do.** Joshua 1:8

The period separating the end of Malachi and the beginning of Matthew is called the “Inter-Testamental Period”. It is a 400-year period in which God did not speak to man through angels or prophets. It was a silent time, not dissimilar to the period of time when Eli was high priest. The Bible tells us in 1 Samuel 3:1, "The boy Samuel served the Lord in Eli’s presence. In those days the word of the Lord was rare and prophetic visions were not widespread." It was uncommon to hear from God and then God elevated Samuel over many years to be a Prophet of God, speaking God's word to His people.

We are living in a day when the world has shut its ears to the Word of God. Yet, that does not eliminate the need or the call from God to proclaim His Word. We are called to sow the seed of God wherever and whenever we can. No farmer would expect a harvest if he never sowed seed. We cannot expect a harvest if we do not proclaim what God has done or is doing in our lives.

I always find amazing that people who do not know the Lord have no problem whatsoever talking about anything at all. But, somehow, we have bought into the idea that we can only mention God when the subject comes up. Why not just be you and when, in the norm, you would say something of a spiritual or godly nature, let it out, don't hold it in? No seed, no harvest. It is such a simple principle but one that we need to be reminded of time and time again.

God's Word is powerful and sharper than any two edged sword (Hebrews 4:12). It is spiritual and not natural and is doing a work far greater than we can see with our natural eyes. Demonic forces dread the sword that you carry. They don't want God's Word brought into any conversation. But we are on the winning side and God backs up His Word with might and with power. Why are we so ashamed of the very words that are spirit and life, healing and wisdom, grace and power to every life?

When we are sincere and genuine, not forceful or pushy but loving and kind, people will gladly hear what we have to say, not only that, they will be the very ones that come to us when they have needs in their lives. Recently, I offered prayer to a young man whose daughter was in hospital with an asthma attack. He desperately wanted her home for Christmas, but he wasn't looking to God. I told him I would pray. He thanked me twice and then, when she made it home Christmas Eve, he sent me a message letting me know and expressing appreciation for my prayers. Seed were sown; God was glorified.

Courage to speak is not always easy and it is little wonder that the apostles prayed for courage to preach. The only difference is that they could lose their lives for preaching. Now if you are living in North America that is not so much an issue. In other countries, however, you could very well forfeit your life for speaking about Jesus. The command to share the living word, Jesus, with others does not go away. Be directed by the Holy Spirit to show the love of God to those around you.

The Dead Sea, located in Israel, is the lowest spot on the earth. It is actually 423 meters below sea level (17) there is beautiful life-giving fresh water flowing from the mountains into the Dead Sea. The only problem is that the Dead Sea has no outlet and so what should be a source of life and blessing is actually filled with such salty water that it is also called the salt sea. You cannot drown in it because you cannot go under the water because of the amount of sediment in the sea. It is called the Dead Sea because there is no aquatic life in it due to its salinity. Because there is no outlet of the life-giving water that is coming in, it has become a place of death.

The same is true for any life that continually receives the Word of God but does not give it away. To know God is to know love. To know love and not love will surely bring death. Love produces love and it produces life, and the same is for our lives when we come into relationship with God. So let the words of life flow out of your life.

*Daddy, I open my mouth and choose to give out of the life that You have given me. I pray for God-incidences, divine opportunities to come my way so I can proclaim who You are. Should I not see them at first, I pray that Your love will compel me to declare Your goodness.*

*17.* Monitoring of the Dead Sea". Israel Marine Data Center (ISRAMAR

## Day 118

## Pray the Word

### Read Ephesians 1:15-19

You are in the Bible. Your life story is recorded there before your very eyes. When you are reading the Bible, you are reading your own story. It was written before you were born but it was written out for you so that you could read it and live it. I know this may sound strange at first, but the simple reality is that the Word of God is the most liberating book in the whole world. It lifts us up beyond where we are and gives us vision for what life was always intended to be.

When I see Moses up on the mountain meeting with God crying out to God, “Show me your Glory!" it resonates in my spirit. My heart cries with him, “Yes Lord, show Me Your Glory!” When Isaiah is translated to heaven and is purified by a live coal placed on his lips and then hears the call of God Almighty, “Who will go for us, who can we send?” I cry with Isaiah, “Here I am! SEND ME!” When Jesus bends down and washes His disciples’ feet, I recognize that He would wash my feet too, as undeserving as I am. And I hear the call, “As I have done to you, now go and do to each other.” When I see the disciples in the upper room praying for the Holy Spirit to come and baptize them, determined not to leave until He comes, I do the same.

God's Word is a living roma of God's desired interaction between Himself and us. It is not meant to be studied with a view for theology and doctrine alone, but for experience and relationship. God’s intention is that when we come to the His Word, we find prayer fuel. It can at times be difficult to pray, but when we come to the Word of God each day, if we are looking for prayer fuel, then every day we will be praying something from the Word. We know that we are praying the will of God so we will have no wonders or worries as to whether or not it will take place.

There is such a great comfort in knowing that when we pray God's Word back to Him, we have the assurance and confidence that He will answer powerfully. The psalmist said that we become what we worship. If you honor and respect and worship what is good, right, holy and true than you will become just like that. But if you revere, praise and exalt selfishness, anger, lust then you will become like that. So it is no wonder when we look into the world around us and see the spirit of rebellion and violence running rampant, it is a result of having exalted those very ideas in front of the nations for decades.

Through prayer, we set the standard of what we want our lives to look like. I want to look like Jesus, and the more time I spend in His presence, declaring His truth and praying His will, the more I will mirror His character and nature into the world.

Jesus taught us to pray for God's Kingdom to come and His will to be done in the earth. We are the answer to that prayer. Romans 6 declares that we are weapons of righteousness when we present ourselves to God as those who are alive from the dead. God's grace enables us to be the transformative power that turns the world right side up. We are the divine influencers in the earth, unlocking the Kingdom of God so that others can come into a living vital relationship with God. To see the earth transformed into a heavenly likeness is only bringing it back to its original purpose and intent.

Saint Augustine said it best: “Pray as if it all depended on God, and work as though it all depended on you." May I simply clarify that John Wesley prayed the mind, heart and will of God for his generation. In knowing God's heart, he revealed it to the nation around him and changed the course of England for generations. Do we dare to believe God for the same?

*Daddy, the whole world becomes a different place when we consider that Your heart so desires to see those that don't know You come to You and be saved. Show me your glory, Lord. Unveil my eyes to see You. Here I am. Send me wherever You choose. I choose to serve as You served and as You continue to serve us out of Your great love for us. Your Kingdom come to the world through me; Your will be done in the earth through me. I am Your ambassador who is filled with Your Holy Spirit to be a world changer just like Jesus is.*

## Day 119

### Praying Bible Prayers

**"For this reason I kneel before the Father from whom every family in heaven and on earth is named. I pray that He may grant you, according to the riches of His glory, to be strengthened with power in the inner man through His Spirit, and that the Messiah may dwell in your hearts through faith. I pray that you, being rooted and firmly established in love, may be able to comprehend with all the saints what is the length and width, height and depth of God's love, and to know the Messiah's love that surpasses knowledge, so you may be filled with all the fullness of God. Now to Him who is able to do above and beyond all that we ask or think according to the power that works in us— to Him be glory in the church and in Christ Jesus to all generations, forever and ever. Amen.** " Ephesians 3:14-21

The Apostle Paul started out as a Pharisee named Saul who was responsible for the death of Stephen. He radically persecuted the Church, considering them a cult of Judaism that was proclaiming heresy to fellow Jews. The intention of his heart was good but his means were wrong and, as he found out later, so was his idea of heresy.

God revealed Himself to Saul and changed his name to Paul. Paul became a fierce proponent of the truth of God while planting church after church after church throughout the Roman Empire. Paul has many apostolic prayers that reveal truths that have the potential to radically transform our thinking and praying. The more we embrace them, the more able we are to live them out in our daily lives.

How do you know something that surpasses knowledge? To the normal mind that is a contradiction. Strengthened with power through His Spirit according to the riches of His glory I can understand what he means, being rooted and firmly established in love, I can see that too. Desiring to comprehend with all the saints the all-encompassing Love of God, wow what a prayer but I can see the significance of crying out for such a revelation. But to know something past knowing.... this is where it gets a little tricky, was it a bad translation, missed interpretation or is Paul saying that it is not something the natural mind cannot conceive of and therefore is something that must be experienced. All the books, counseling and sermons in the world on the love of God will not make a difference in someone's life. The change comes when it goes from their head to their heart, when it is no longer a doctrine but an experience.

When Jesus showed up on the road to Damascus, Saul was blinded by His glory. When God spoke to Him and revealed "I am Jesus whom You are persecuting", Saul went into an immediate fast without food or water as the reality of the revelation began to sink in. Saul was radically transformed as all the i's were dotted and t's were crossed in his great mind as he began to understand that this Jesus of Nazareth was the long awaited for Messiah. God had been faithful to His people. He fulfilled His promises that started on the day of the fall and had been spoken of down through history. Saul's mind must have been rattled as the fullness of these truths all added up to the great love of God for humanity revealed in the cross of Christ. His own lips declared that it was the love of God that compelled him to do all that he did and to endure all that he endured.

*Daddy, let me never move from the significance of Your love. Let me always be filled with more and more of Your great love. Let my heart be filled with compassion for the lost and let hunger and thirst for more of Your love be seen in me. Let me experience waves of Your love. "O the deep, deep love of Jesus, vast, unmeasured, boundless, free, rolling as a mighty ocean in its fullness over me."*

## Day 120

### Praying the Word

**For this reason also, since the day we heard this, we haven't stopped praying for you. We are asking that you may be filled with the knowledge of His will in all wisdom and spiritual understanding, so that you may walk worthy of the Lord, fully pleasing to Him, bearing fruit in every good work and growing in the knowledge of God. May you be strengthened with all power, according to His glorious might, for all endurance and patience, with joy giving thanks to the Father, who has enabled you to share in the saints' inheritance in the light. He has rescued us from the domain of darkness and transferred us into the kingdom of the Son He loves. We have redemption, the forgiveness of sins, in Him.** Colossians 1:9-14

Through Paul's letter to the Colossians, the Spirit of God is writing to you and to me. God wants us to be filled with the knowledge of His will in all wisdom and spiritual understanding so that we may walk worthy and pleasing to Him, prosperous in God's work and growing in knowing God intimately. It is one thing to know the will of God and yet another to have the wisdom and understanding of how God works it out in and through our lives. Israel knew God's acts but Moses knew His ways. (Psalm 103:7) It does not take much to know God's will in abstaining from sin, living righteously, being a witness and having a servant's heart. But living it out when all hell is breaking loose against you is where we need the wisdom and spiritual understanding of God. I love the statement that God desires that we be strengthened with all power according to His glorious might.

His might is not for external displays of power, although those have their place. It is so that we might have power for endurance and patience, giving thanks with joy to Daddy God for who He is. The Father has it all under control even though at times it might not seem like it. There are times in our lives when trouble may be on every side, it is then that we need to know that power is available for us. We need to keep putting our trust in God even when it is the darkest, when money has run out and bills have piled up, when persecution has come because you have been the devils worst nightmare. Grace to endure is available when you feel that everything is turning out wrong. God says He makes all things work together for our good. All things include the negative things, the wrong things, the hurtful things, the failures and the sins. God can make all things work together for our good when we say yes to His purposes and plans and not our own.

*Daddy, Your plans are perfect, although I can't always see that. You know what You are doing, perfecting us, shaping us, moulding us into the image of Your Son. I thank You for the power to endure patiently with joy in thanksgiving for who You are and what You will reveal in Your timing.*

## Day 121

## Praying the Word

"And I pray this: that your love will keep on growing in knowledge and every kind of discernment, [10] so that you can approve the things that are superior and can be pure and blameless in the day of Christ, [11] filled with the fruit of righteousness that comes through Jesus Christ to the glory and praise of God." Phil. 1:9-11

In closing this section of the book, this being the last day before we start a new series in the New Believer's Devotional, we see some very unique themes running through Paul's prayers. He speaks of love, growing, knowledge, fruitfulness and the glory of God. Jesus made it crystal clear in John 15 that He desires that our lives be fruitful. God will work like any farmer to ensure that fruitfulness is the end result of our lives.

A term that is very popular today is "leaving a legacy behind"—not just an inheritance, but a legacy. Long after you are dead and gone, the impact of your life is still being felt. The influence that you carried is still notable because it was so powerful and beneficial to all who knew you. Your significance is still remembered and honored generations after you are dead. That is a legacy we should all seek to have. Not we lived, procreated, left money and died. Lives that encountered our lives should be changed, impacted for eternity because they knew us. Bondages should be broken in people's lives, marriages healed, relationships restored, lives filled with purpose and even nations healed through the influence of godly men and women. That is the vision that God has for His Church.

Through Paul, God is teaching us to pray that we would "approve the things that are superior". In other words, there are things with which we can be involved that are inferior--not sins or things that are immoral, but simply things that are inferior, less significant and of lesser importance that prevent us from doing what is superior, of greater significance and of higher importance.

We need to grow in knowledge and discernment so we can look at our lives and answer the question, "Am I doing what is significant or what is insignificant? Is what I am working toward truly what God would call superior or is it what God would call an inferior use of my time, talents and finances? What am I building? Will it last the judgment or will it burn when it is tried with God's fire?" This will surely lead to being pure and blameless on the day of Christ which is in reference to the Judgment Seat of Christ for the believer. This is not a judgement as to whether we are saved or not, but a reckoning for our actions after Christ came into our lives. The actions done in our body, not what we prayed, not what was in our heart to do, but what did we actually do. When we see our lives from the light of eternity, it sheds a different perspective on what is superior and what is inferior.

As we end this season of devotion and we look in the mirror of our lives, what do we see that needs to change? It goes without saying that the things that are superior in life are the things of the Spirit and of the Kingdom, such as the proclamation of the gospel, living selflessly instead of selfishly, choosing to be a servant no matter what position of responsibility you are in, loving everybody equally. The list could go on and on so the challenge in discerning is what is God putting His finger on in this season of your life? Be ready to respond in worshipful obedience.

*Daddy thank You for this season of growth and transformation in my life. I see You more clearly now than I did before and I pray that I would continually discern in my life the things that are of superior quality, leading me to stand before You in glorious expectation.*

## Week Four

1. What should our one goal and primary purpose be in our relationship with God?

2. "God's word is a living picture of …….?"

3. Who is the greatest interpreter of the Word?

4. Romans 8:28 says that God makes all things work together for our good, what are some of the 'all things' do you think God is referring too? What are the two conditions upon which this applies to a life? Do you fulfill those conditions?

5. Quote last week's verse and memorize Romans 8:28

CPSIA information can be obtained
at www.ICGtesting.com
Printed in the USA
LVHW05s0125020518
575637LV00001B/20/P

9 781927 684139